PARACLETE

The Spirit of Truth in the Church

FR. ANDREW APOSTOLI, C.F.R.

SERVANT
BOOKS

PUBLISHED BY ST. ANTHONY MESSENGER PRESS
CINCINNATI, OHIO

RESCRIPT

In accord with the *Code of Canon Law*, I hereby grant my permission to publish *Paraclete: The Spirit of Truth in the Church* written by Andrew Apostoli.

Most Reverend Daniel E. Pilarczyk
Archbishop of Cincinnati
Cincinnati, Ohio
June 2, 2005

Permission to publish is a declaration that a book or pamphlet is considered to be free of doctrinal or moral error. It is not implied that those who have granted the permission to publish agree with the contents, opinions or statements expressed.

Unless otherwise noted, Scripture passages have been taken from the *Revised Standard Version*, Catholic edition. Copyright 1946, 1952, 1971 by the Division of Christian Education of the National Council of Churches of Christ in the USA. Used by permission. All rights reserved.
Excerpts from the *Catechism of the Catholic Church* have been taken from the second edition, copyright ©1994, 1997, United States Catholic Conference.
Excerpts from canon law are taken from *Code of Canon Law*, Latin-English translation (Washington: Canon Law Society of America, 1998).
Excerpts from Vatican II Documents are taken from Austin P. Flannery, ed., *Documents of Vatican II* (Grand Rapids, Mich.: Eerdmans, 1978).

Cover photo illustration by Steve Eames
Photo: ©Imagemore/SuperStock
Book design by Phillips Robinette, O.F.M.

Library of Congress Cataloging-in-Publication Data

Apostoli, Andrew.
   Paraclete : the spirit of truth in the church / Andrew Apostoli.
      p. cm.
   Includes index.
   ISBN 0-86716-717-3 (pbk. : alk. paper) 1. Holy Spirit. 2. Catholic Church—Doctrines. 3. Jesus—Person and offices. I. Title.

BT121.3.A66 2005
231'.3—dc22
                    2005012100

ISBN 0-86716-717-3
Copyright ©2005 Andrew Apostoli. All rights reserved.

Published by Servant Books, an imprint of St. Anthony Messenger Press
28 W. Liberty St.
Cincinnati, OH 45202
www.AmericanCatholic.org

Printed in the United States of America

Printed on acid-free paper

05 06 07 08 09 5 4 3 2 1

This book is lovingly and gratefully dedicated to the
Blessed Virgin Mary, Spouse of the Holy Spirit
and Mother of the Church,
as well as to the late Pope John Paul II who,
under the direction of the Holy Spirit
led the Church into the third millennium,
and to his successor Pope Benedict XVI who has the
awesome task of shepherding God's people and
spreading the message of Christ throughout the world.

Acknowledgments

This book could only have been completed through the blessing of the Most Holy Trinity. I am filled with great gratitude to Almighty God and I pray that this book will redound to the honor and glory of the Father, the Son and the Holy Spirit!

I also wish to thank the Blessed Virgin Mary, the Mother of the Church and the first and most important disciple of Jesus. Without her beautiful intercession this book would never have become a reality.

I would also like to thank two special people who helped in the production of this work. First, my thanks to Mary Majkowski who very patiently typed this book as it went through a number of revisions and frequently had to encourage the author to complete the task. Second, I want to thank Fr. Benedict Groeschel, C.F.R., the author's confrere, for so kindly preparing the foreword for this book.

I also wish to acknowledge and thank Servant Books for accepting the manuscript for publication, and Cindy Cavnar, its editor, for invaluable assistance in preparing the text for publication.

Contents

FOREWORD

You might wonder why we need another book on the Holy Spirit. And the simple answer is that you can never get too much on the Holy Spirit. Fr. Andrew Apostoli stresses the Holy Spirit's impact on the Church through its history and as the Church fulfills its role in the world today.

Many of us have been concerned and even troubled by confusion in Christian teachings in the last decades of the twentieth century. Some have wondered out loud if the Holy Spirit has left us! The very recent events surrounding the death of Pope John Paul II and the election of Pope Benedict XVI have demonstrated again that the Holy Spirit is presiding over the Church. In fact, any student of history could recognize in the remarkable survival and growth of the Catholic Church that the hand of God has obviously been there. Divine guidance and providence work through the Holy Spirit in this world. He passes over the dark waters of human history and brings life and peace where there would be turmoil and chaos.

As always, Fr. Andrew brings an informed and prayerful light to this mystery of grace. If you are a longstanding Fr. Andrew fan, you will enjoy this book. If you are a new reader, you will be in for a treat.

Fr. Benedict Groeschel, C.F.R.
April, 2005

PART I

Jesus Gives Us the Truth;
the Spirit Helps Us
Understand It

CHAPTER 1

The Mission of Jesus and His Church: To Proclaim the Truth

THE HEART OF THE CATHOLIC FAITH is the belief that Jesus Christ, the Son of God, became man so that He might in turn become the Savior of the world. The Church's sacred tradition clearly teaches this. In the Nicene Creed, for example, we proclaim that Jesus came down from heaven "for us men and for our salvation."

Sacred Scripture also makes this clear. Throughout the Gospels Our Lord expressed the purpose of His coming in very specific ways. For example, He told the Pharisees, who criticized Him for eating with tax collectors and public sinners, that He had come precisely to call such sinners—not the self-righteous—to salvation (see Matthew 9:13).

On another occasion He compared His own religious leadership over the people with that of the Pharisees. The Pharisees exercised leadership as would thieves or hired hands. They stole from the flock for self-gain, and in the face of danger they fled, showing no concern for the flock but only for themselves. In contrast, Jesus exercised leadership as a shepherd caring for his flock of sheep. He said of Himself that He had come to give His people "life…abundantly" and that, like a good shepherd, He would lay down His life for His sheep (see John 10:10–11).

Jesus' passion presents yet another reason why He came into the world, a reason related directly to the theme of truth. In fact, the Passion focuses on the profound conflict between good and evil or, more precisely, between truth and anti-truth. The conflict emerges with dramatic intensity during the trial of Jesus before the Roman procurator Pontius Pilate.

REJECTION BY THE RELIGIOUS LEADERS

Jesus was tried and condemned first by corrupt religious leaders who had closed their hearts to the truth. They had refused time and again to look at reality, at the record regarding Jesus. In the hardness of their hearts they refused to consider the goodness of His conduct, His compassionate forgiveness of sinners, His constant pity in healing the sick, the stupendous "signs" He had worked, including raising the dead back to life. He Himself said, "Even though you do not believe me, believe the works" (John 10:38). But they would not.

Jesus met this opposition throughout His public ministry. Although He entered a world that had awaited Him for centuries, few received Him and most rejected Him. Saint John points out that the basic reason Jesus and His truth were rejected was the opposition of anti-truth: Satan, the deceiver, the father of lies, continually opposed the truth of Jesus.

This comes out clearly in Jesus' dialogues with the people, especially with the Jewish leaders at the time. Part of that dialogue ran:

> Jesus then said to the Jews who had believed in him, "If you continue in my word, you are truly my disciples, and you will know the truth, and the truth will make you free." They answered him, "We are descendants of Abraham, and have never been in bondage to anyone.[1]
>
> How is it that you say, 'You will be made free'?" Jesus answered them, "Truly, truly, I say to you, every one who commits sin is a slave to sin.... I know that you are descendants of Abraham; yet you seek to kill me, because my word finds no place in you. I speak of what I have seen with my Father, and you do what you have heard from your father." They answered him, "Abraham is our father."
>
> Jesus said to them, "If you were Abraham's children, you would do what Abraham did, but now you seek to kill me, a man who has told you the truth which I heard from God; this is not what Abraham did. You do what your father did." They said to him, "We were not born of fornication; we have one Father, even God."
>
> Jesus said to them, "If God were your Father, you would love me, for I proceeded and came forth from God; I came not of my own accord, but he sent me. Why do you not understand what I say? It is because you cannot bear to hear my word. You are of your father the devil, and your will is to do your father's desires. He was a murderer from the beginning, and has nothing to do with the truth, because there is no truth in him. When he lies, he speaks according to his own nature, for he is a liar and the father of lies. But, because I tell the truth, you do not believe me.

"Which of you convicts me of sin? If I tell the truth, why do you not believe me? He who is of God hears the words of God; the reason why you do not hear them is that you are not of God."

—JOHN 8:31–34, 37–47

The hearts of the people, especially those of the leaders, were closed tightly against Jesus. He didn't "fit their mold" for the Messiah, so He had to go. The blinding deceit of the anti-truth prejudiced them against the truth. Any one of them might have said to Jesus, "I've got my mind made up; don't disturb me with the facts."

REJECTION BY THE SECULAR POWERS

The religious court sought to have Jesus put to death, so they sent Him to the civil authority, the Roman procurator Pontius Pilate. We can assume that Pilate had heard a great deal about Jesus; after all, Jesus had caused quite a stir during the three years of His public ministry. No doubt Pilate had heard rumors of a kingdom Jesus had promised His followers.

Pilate asked Jesus if He was a king. Jesus responded that His kingdom "is not of this world."

Pilate said to him, "So you are a king?" Jesus answered, "You say that I am a king. For this I was born, and for this I have come into the world, to bear witness to the truth. Every one who is of the truth hears my voice." Pilate said to him, "What is truth?"

—JOHN 18:37–38

What a contrast we have here in the attitudes of Jesus and of Pilate with regard to the truth. Jesus says that truth is so important that the very reason He came into the world was to bear witness to the truth—to the "living and true God" (see 1 Thessalonians 1:9). He had come to bear witness to the fact that, as the Gospel of John says, He alone is "the way, and the truth, and the life" (14:6), "the resurrection and the life" (11:25), "the living bread which came down from heaven" (6:51), "the light of the world" (8:12), "the good shepherd" (10:14), the Son of God and Savior of all mankind.

Can anything be more important than to know, believe, love and live this truth about Jesus in order to receive the eternal life He promised? This is the truth that allows us to become free, not with a freedom for license but with the glorious freedom to be what we have been created to be. It is the freedom of the children of God (see Romans 8:21).

How different the attitude of Pilate! One can almost hear the sneering and sarcasm in his retort: "What is truth?" He didn't know, and he couldn't have cared less. He only knew and cared about the job he had to do: to preserve Roman sovereignty supreme and unchallenged. This included maintaining law and order, no matter what the cost and no matter who paid the price.

We must admit that Pilate did give Jesus a fair hearing. Three times he pronounced Jesus innocent (see John 18:38; 19:4; 19:6): "I find no crime in him." But he lost his sense of justice when his reputation and career advancement were threatened. He heard the people shout: "If you release this man, you are not Caesar's friend; every one who makes himself a king sets himself against Caesar" (John 19:12). Feeling pressured to be politically correct, he flip-flopped on the issue. Since he scorned real truth, truth became whatever he wanted it to be. He ended up condemning Jesus despite stating that Jesus was innocent.

People can easily lead conflicting lives: believing one thing but doing another. Pilate could have gone down in history as a hero, the one who set Jesus free; instead we remember him sadly every time we profess in the Creed that Jesus "suffered under Pontius Pilate." And how did his flip-flop on the truth further his career in politics and government? According to tradition, the capricious Roman Emperor Caligula later removed Pilate from office. The world's favor and popularity quickly pass.

TRUTH TODAY

The Church continues today to speak the truth of Christ. This is her mission until the end of time, until Jesus comes in glory to verify all that has been said of Him and to bring to fulfillment all that He has promised.

The secular world, on the other hand, continues to oppose the message of the Church. God and His law are increasingly removed from the social scene. Jesus foretold this opposition when He said that if we belonged to the world, the world would love us as its own. But because He has called us "out of the world"—not to live by its distorted values but by what He has taught us—the world hates us (see John 15:18–19).

The world has many resources in its secular governments, media, people of wealth and power and prestige. The resources of the Church, in comparison, seem so inadequate, like the five barley loaves and two fish to feed the crowd of five thousand who had come to hear Jesus: "What are they among so many?" (see John 6:9). But the Lord did not leave us alone: He gave the gift whose presence enables the Church to the end of time to proclaim that "Jesus is Lord" (see 1 Corinthians 12:3). He has given us the gift of the Spirit of truth, to be with His Church always! ✒

CHAPTER 2

Our Need for the Spirit of Truth

ACCORDING TO AN OLD SAYING, hindsight is 20/20 vision. This means that we often fail to appreciate the full impact of decisions and events in our lives until they have run their course. Their end serves as a vantage point from which we can look back and realize the meaning and significance of those events.

Something of this sort occurred in the lives of the apostles. They had been with Our Lord for the three years of His public life. They had heard His preaching, seen His miracles and even shared His Last Supper. They had come to believe in Him. Simon Peter, who was to become the prince of the apostles, had been the spokesman for their faith. He proclaimed Jesus as the long-awaited Messiah:

> Now when Jesus came into the district of Caesarea Philippi, he asked his disciples, "Who do men say that the Son of Man is?" And they said, "Some say John the Baptist, others say Elijah, and others Jeremiah or one of the prophets." He said to them, "But who do you say that I am?" Simon Peter replied, "You are the Christ, the Son of the living God."
>
> —MATTHEW 16:13–16

Again, when Jesus declared Himself to be "the bread which comes down from heaven" and promised to give His flesh and blood for our food and drink (see John 6:48–58), Simon Peter proclaimed the apostles' steadfast loyalty to Jesus as the crowds walked away from Him: "Jesus said to the twelve, 'Will you also go away?' Simon Peter answered him, 'Lord, to whom shall we go? You have the words of eternal life; and we have believed, and have come to know, that you are the Holy One of God'" (John 6:67–69).

But then came those unexpected—more accurately, unthinkable—events of Holy Thursday night and Good Friday. Despite his protests at the Last Supper that he was ready to die for Jesus, Simon Peter, in his weakness, denied Him three times (see Luke 22:54–62). The other apostles didn't do very well either. In fact, they fled for their lives in panic (see Matthew 26:56).

These events were bad enough, but the ultimate tragedy seemed to be Jesus' crucifixion and death. Who can describe the disciples' profound sorrow over these events? How shattered and disillusioned they must have felt! Was He not the Messiah? What about the hopes they thought would be fulfilled in Him?

This sorrow and confusion is clearly evident in the two disciples who walked with heavy hearts on the road from Jerusalem to Emmaus that Easter Sunday morning:

> That very day two of them were going to a village named Emmaus, about seven miles from Jerusalem, and talking with each other about all these things that had happened. While they were talking and discussing together, Jesus himself drew near and went with them.

But their eyes were kept from recognizing him. And he said to them, "What is this conversation which you are holding with each other as you walk?" And they stood still, looking sad. Then one of them, named Cleopas, answered him, "Are you the only visitor to Jerusalem who does not know the things that have happened there in these days?" And he said to them, "What things?" And they said to him, "Concerning Jesus of Nazareth, who was a prophet mighty in deed and word before God and all the people, and how our chief priests and rulers delivered him up to be condemned to death, and crucified him. But we had hoped that he was the one to redeem Israel."

—LUKE 24:13–21

After the tragic events of Jesus' suffering and death, the disciples and apostles needed a vantage point from which to look back and try to grasp more clearly what Jesus had said about who He was and about the true meaning of His mission, especially regarding His passion and death. At the same time, they needed a new and more powerful light of truth to enable them to comprehend the fullness of the mystery of Christ, their Lord and Savior.

God would provide both the vantage point and the light. The New Testament records two critical events that equipped the apostles and disciples to understand the truth about Jesus' identity, mission and message.

THE POWER OF CHRIST'S RESURRECTION

The first great event was Our Lord's resurrection from the dead on Easter Sunday. This was the vantage point from which those first disciples could view Jesus' life and death in a new light. They realized that Jesus' life did not end abruptly in tragic, unforeseen events. Rather, He was in full control of His destiny, as He Himself had actually declared: "For this reason the Father loves me, because I lay down my life, that I may take it again. No one takes it from me, but I lay it down of my own accord. I have power to lay it down, and I have power to take it again; this charge I have received from my Father" (John 10:17–18).

Looking at Jesus' death after His resurrection, the disciples realized that He freely accepted the Father's will to suffer and die for the salvation of the world. They understood that Jesus' death was not an unavoidable tragedy in the face of which Jesus had been helpless; instead, it was the greatest act of love the world had ever seen. They came to realize that the God who had become man, that the Creator who took on the nature of His own creature, died for their sins. What unspeakable love! Had He not said that there could be no greater love than for a person to "lay down his life for his friends" (see John 15:13)?

But there was more. Through His death Jesus conquered sin by atoning for our sins. Through His resurrection He conquered death by destroying the power His own death seemed to have over Him. Now, in turn, He holds out to all humanity the promise of bodily resurrection and eternal life.

During Jesus' lifetime the disciples thought of Him as a messiah who would drive out the Romans from their nation and restore the earthly kingdom of David. They now could see that He had freed them from the greater tyranny of sin and Satan and the fear of eternal punishment. They now realized that He was preparing for them a heavenly kingdom, which He won for them by His saving death. If all they had hoped for previously in Christ would have come to an end with their bodily death, how much greater was their joy now in the hope of eternal life!

No wonder Saint Paul could teach so boldly about the glorification of our bodies at the resurrection on the last day:

> For the trumpet will sound, and the dead will be raised imperishable, and we shall be changed. For this perishable nature must put on the imperishable, and this mortal nature must put on immortality. When the perishable puts on the imperishable, and the mortal puts on immortality, then shall come to pass the saying that is written: "Death is swallowed up in victory." "O death, where is thy victory? O death, where is thy sting?" …But thanks be to God, who gives us the victory through Our Lord Jesus Christ.
>
> —1 CORINTHIANS 15:52–55, 57

The resurrection of Jesus, then, provided His first disciples with the standard by which they could judge the true meaning of His life and mission, culminating in His death on the cross for the salvation of the world.

THE SPIRIT COMES ON PENTECOST

The disciples still needed an intense spiritual light to help them penetrate the mysteries of who Jesus was and what He taught about His kingdom. The second great event recorded in the New Testament provided this light: the coming of the Holy Spirit on Pentecost.

Through the Spirit's coming the apostles received a deeper understanding of all that Jesus said and did. This strengthened the conviction of the first Christians that Jesus was both "Lord and Christ," as Peter himself proclaimed on that first Pentecost (see Acts 2:36). The Scriptures detail the apostles' need for the Spirit of truth.

To Overcome Fear

In the time between the Resurrection and Pentecost, it was evident that the apostles were in need of further spiritual help! For one thing, they were full of fear. Saint John tells us that immediately after Jesus' death, the apostles feared that the Jewish authorities would seek them out and punish them as disciples of Our Lord: "...the doors of the house where the disciples had met were locked for fear of the Jews" (see John 20:19, NRSV).

This fear on the part of the apostles was understandable. After all, it was early Easter night, and Jesus had not yet appeared to them. But one week later, even after they had seen the risen Lord, they were still hiding in the Upper Room with the doors securely bolted (see John 20:26). This would not have been the case if they had already reached spiritual maturity. As one's love grows perfect, all fear of suffering is removed. As Saint John wrote: "There is no fear in love, but perfect love casts out fear. For fear has to do with punishment, and he who fears is not perfected in love" (1 John 4:18).

The apostles had actually grown stronger in their faith and trust even though they needed further growth. On Holy Thursday night they fled in absolute panic the moment Jesus was seized. Now, after the Resurrection, at least they were no longer running away. They had begun to change for the better.

But how would they overcome their remaining fear? This would be the work of the Spirit of truth. When He came on Pentecost, the Paraclete taught them that Jesus' victory over suffering and death would be their victory also. They no longer needed to be afraid. Now they could go out and boldly proclaim Jesus' resurrection even to the Jewish authorities they had feared so much on Holy Thursday. Clearly, it was not until the Spirit of truth came that the apostles could grasp these things and be free from fear.

To Correct Misunderstandings

Sacred Scripture gives us another indication of the apostles' lack of perfection, revealed in their questions and statements. These demonstrate a lingering misunderstanding about much of what Jesus had taught them.

At the Last Supper Jesus promised to send the Spirit of truth. He told His apostles they needed the Spirit because they were suffering from spiritual dullness, the inability to understand and appreciate the deeper realities He wanted to teach them: "I have yet many things to say to you, but you cannot bear them now" (John 16:12).

Although they had been in Our Lord's company for three years, the apostles still had only very limited spiritual capacity. They didn't realize the full importance of Jesus' life; Scripture tells us that they couldn't grasp His divinity despite His efforts to enlighten them. They missed the meaning and implication of many of His teachings, especially those dealing with His approaching death and resurrection. Their need for the Spirit of truth continued even after Easter. Despite their having the vantage point of Jesus' resurrection, they were still far from the spiritual insight and perfection Jesus desired for them.

Our Lord pointed out to His apostles how this difficulty would be remedied: "When the Spirit of truth comes, he will guide you into all the truth" (John 16:13). It was the Holy Spirit's role to give the apostles fuller spiritual understanding. He would enlighten their minds and stir their hearts, especially regarding the meaning of the Lord's passion and resurrection, once these events had taken place. He would help them to see their own role in the hidden plan of God for the salvation of the world.

At the Last Supper Our Lord stated this precise work of the Holy Spirit: "These things I have spoken to you, while I am still with you. But the Counselor, the Holy Spirit, whom the Father will send in my name, he will teach you all things, and bring to your remembrance all that I have said to you" (John 14:25–26, emphasis mine). The verb that Jesus used here—*to remind* or *to recall* or *to bring to remembrance*— was a technical term. It did not mean simply to recall historical events or facts that were now part of a historical record. Rather it meant to *appreciate* more fully in the present what had been said or done in the past. It meant *grasping* the deeper meaning that these past words or deeds held for the present and even the future.

Finally, it meant to *experience* these past truths and realities as living and acting among them even in the present moment. So when Jesus said the Holy Spirit will bring to remembrance, He was telling the apostles that the Spirit would give them insight into the meaning of His words and deeds and show them how important these words and deeds would become in their own lives.

An Example: The Temple and the Body of Christ

Saint John gives a clear example of this when he describes Jesus' cleansing the temple (see John 2:13–22). On that occasion Jesus came into the temple and encountered a scene that stirred His righteous anger. He saw moneychangers doing a lively business and groups of animals— "oxen and sheep and pigeons"—gathered in the precincts of the temple. In His zeal for the dignity of the temple—"my Father's house"—He overturned the moneychangers' tables and drove the animals out.

In reaction to what must have been quite a spectacle, the Jewish authorities demanded of Our Lord a sign showing He had authority to do such a thing. They must have been thinking something like, "Who does He think He is, coming to the temple and doing such a thing?"

"'Destroy this temple,' was Jesus' answer, 'and in three days I will raise it up'" (John 2:19). At the time the temple in Jerusalem was still being built. So the Jews objected, telling Jesus that the temple had been under construction for forty-six years and it still was not finished; how could He possibly rebuild it in three days?

Saint John reveals the deeper meaning of Jesus' words: "But he spoke of the temple of his body. When therefore he was raised from the dead, his disciples *remembered* that he had said this; and they believed the scripture and the word which Jesus had spoken" (John 2:21–22, emphasis mine).

Here we see the verb *to remember.* The apostles understood clearly after Jesus' resurrection that He was not talking about rebuilding the temple in Jerusalem made of stone. During the period of the old covenant, God's spiritual presence dwelt in the Holy of Holies of that stone temple. But the old covenant ended with the death of Jesus on the cross. The stone temple no longer had any purpose! Jesus' own body was the new "temple," where God in the fullness of His divinity would dwell among His people. Thus the old covenant temple of stone was replaced with the new covenant temple of Jesus' own flesh and blood. Jesus, in rising from the dead, "rebuilt" the temple, the temple of His own body.

John tells us further that the disciples came to believe the Scripture (Jesus had quoted Psalm 69:9: "For zeal for thy house has consumed me") and "the word which Jesus had spoken." The disciples placed Jesus' spoken word on the same level as the inspired written Word of God in Scripture. They now recognized Jesus as speaking with divine authority. This realization was the result of the Spirit's coming to them, the Spirit of truth.

OUR FAITH STILL RESTS ON EASTER AND PENTECOST
We have so much to be thankful for as we live our Catholic faith today. Like the apostles, we have the vantage point of Jesus' resurrection to help us grasp who He really is and His importance for our lives. As Saint Paul wrote to his converts at Corinth: "If Christ has not been raised [from the dead], your faith is futile and you are still in your sins. Then those also who have fallen asleep in Christ have perished. If for this life only we have hoped in Christ, we are of all men most to be pitied" (1 Corinthians 15:17–19).

We also are blessed with the Spirit of truth in the Church and in our personal lives. With the help of His gifts and inspirations, we are able to grasp the fuller meaning of all that

Jesus gives us. The Paraclete opens our minds and hearts to the beauty and power of Sacred Scripture when we read it in a prayerful and reflective manner. He helps us grow in understanding and appreciating the many revealed doctrines preserved and taught in the Catholic Church. As Jesus promised, He leads us into all truth, guiding us to attain the fullness of life Jesus has prepared for us in His heavenly Father's kingdom!

Part II

The Spirit of Truth and His Mission in the Church

Chapter 3

Jesus Promises the Spirit of Truth

THE ACCOUNT OF THE LAST SUPPER in the Gospel of John is among the most beautiful passages in Scripture. The evangelist begins his description with this marvelous statement: "Now before the feast of the Passover, when Jesus knew that his hour had come to depart out of this world to the Father, having loved his own who were in the world, he loved them to the end" (John 13:1).

Jesus would love His own "to the end." What does that mean? Certainly it means to the end of His earthly life, soon to come to a close on the cross. But the expression probably also meant to the end of all His power and His love, of all He could do for us, of all He could give us. Saint John, the disciple "whom Jesus loved" (see John 13:23), with his characteristic spiritual depth and unction, presents to us so many of the treasures Jesus shared in His last meal with His disciples:[1]

☞ His commandment to love one another as He had loved us (see John 15:12)

☞ His example of humble service in washing the feet of His disciples (see 13:3–15)

☞ His joy (see 15:11)

☞ His promise of union with Him, like branches on the vine (see 15:1–8)

☞ His peace (see 14:27)

☞ His promise to prepare a place for us (see 14:3)

☞ His promise to come back again to take us with Him (see 14:18)

☞ His promise of making His home along with the Father within those who love Him and keep His commandments (see 14:23)

☞ and His promise that the prayers of those who ask anything of the Father in His name will be heard (see 16:23)

Without doubt, however, the treasure Jesus promised over and over again at the Last Supper is the Holy Spirit. Four times in Saint John's account Jesus refers to the Holy Spirit as the "Paraclete" (John 14:16, 26; 15:26; 16:7) and three of those times also as the "Spirit of truth" (John 14:17; 15:26; 16:13).[2] In a way these references sound almost like a job description for the role of the Spirit of truth. Let's look at these passages[3] to reflect on what Jesus says the Spirit will do when He comes.

FIRST REFERENCE TO THE HOLY SPIRIT

"I shall ask the Father and he will give you another Paraclete to be with you for ever, the Spirit of truth whom the world can never accept, since it neither sees nor knows him; but you know him, because he is with you, he is in you" (John 14:16–17, NJB).

Another Paraclete to Be with You Always

In this first reference to the Holy Spirit, Jesus calls Him the "Paraclete." Paraclete comes from two Greek words that mean "someone called to one's side," a companion. Most often it referred to a lawyer or advocate. If you are going to court, you want your lawyer at your side!

It is interesting that Jesus refers to the Holy Spirit as "another" Paraclete. This implies a previous Paraclete, which can refer only to Jesus Himself. He has been the companion of the apostles, and now He is going to leave them. But Jesus describes the Holy Spirit, the other Paraclete, as one who will "be with you for ever."

The contrast is sharp and clear. Jesus' mission was soon to be over. He would redeem the world by His death and resurrection and would ascend to His place of glory at the right hand of His heavenly Father, to await His triumphant return at the end of the world. The mission of the Holy Spirit, however, will not end until the Church is complete at the end of time. He will be with us always, carrying out His unseen mission for the salvation and sanctification of the Church until Jesus returns in glory.[4]

Jesus repeats this point for emphasis: the Holy Spirit will remain with us. His mission in each of our lives is not over until our sojourn on earth ends and the Father calls us to His heavenly kingdom. Until death, then, it is important that we remain united spiritually with God, never letting ourselves be separated from Him by mortal sin. Nor must we ever allow our relationship with Him to be weakened by deliberate venial sin. An old saying puts it: "If you are not as close to God now as you were five years ago, you know who moved!"

The Spirit of Truth, Whom the World Cannot Accept

This is Jesus' first reference to the Holy Spirit as the Spirit of truth. He tells us "the world can never accept" the Spirit. "The world" here refers to people whose lives are based on the values and pleasures of this world alone. This worldly attitude is especially evident today in society's attempts to exclude God and His revelation from daily life, or at least to neglect them. Worldly persons cannot be open to the Spirit of truth, since they do not see Him. Worldly people reject those things that demand faith because, for them, seeing is believing; unseen spiritual realities count for nothing.

Another reason the world cannot accept the Spirit of truth, Jesus says, is because it does not know Him. Jesus once compared the Holy Spirit to the wind. We don't see the wind, but we know it from its effects and from the sounds it makes (see John 3:8). In a similar way, we don't know the Holy Spirit directly but only through His effects in our lives; we recognize Him through His "fruits."

Saint Paul tells us that the cravings of the flesh are directly opposed to the fruits of the Spirit (see Galatians 5:16–26). Those given over to the desires of the flesh are unable to recognize the beauty and importance of the spiritual realities toward which the Spirit leads us. Only those who belong to Christ Jesus and have mortified the desires of the flesh have the interior freedom to recognize and desire what the Spirit is doing. Unlike "the world," the apostles belong to Christ and thus recognize the Spirit of truth.

He Will Be Within You

The mission of the Spirit of truth is hidden. For this reason Pope John Paul II referred to the Holy Spirit as "the Hidden God" who is truly with us. Saint Paul reminds us that our bodies are temples of the Holy Spirit who dwells within us (see 1 Corinthians 6:19–20). And He is by no means idle in the soul. He guides us individually—as He guides the whole Church collectively— to accomplish the Father's will on earth as Jesus did. At the same time He is actively forming Christ in us (see Galatians 4:19), helping us to transform our thoughts, words and deeds into a greater likeness to Jesus.

For our part, we must learn to recognize His authentic inspirations. We do this by deepening our prayer life; there, in silence, we hear His voice. We must also foster purity of heart, detaching ourselves from sin and growing in our love and service of God. The Holy Spirit can act freely in a heart that is pure.

SECOND REFERENCE TO THE HOLY SPIRIT

"I have said these things to you while still with you; but the Paraclete, the Holy Spirit, whom the Father will send in my name, will teach you everything and remind you of all I have said to you" (John 14:25–26, NJB).

Whom the Father Will Send in My Name

All the good gifts Jesus won for us by His saving death come ultimately from our heavenly Father. Of these, the Holy Spirit is the gift of God par excellence! Jesus Himself had referred to the Holy Spirit's coming as "the promise of the Father" (see Acts 1:4). In yet another reference to the Holy Spirit's coming from the Father, Jesus told the apostles that they would be "clothed with power from on high" (see Luke 24:49).

The apostles spent the nine days between Ascension Thursday and Pentecost Sunday "devoted to prayer," in company with Our Lady, Jesus' brethren and some of His women followers (see Acts 1:14). (This nine-day period of prayer is generally considered the first novena in the Church.) No doubt they remembered Our Lord's teaching on the need to pray to God the Father to send His Holy Spirit: "If you, then, who are evil, know how to give good gifts to your children, how much more will the heavenly Father give the Holy Spirit to those who ask him" (Luke 11:13).

He Will Instruct You in Everything

The Spirit of truth would teach the apostles "everything," enabling them to grasp in depth all that Jesus had taught. This instruction would affect their hearts as well as their minds. Not only would they receive clearer understanding and greater insight, but they would experience in their hearts the conviction of these truths, the joy of living them and the ardent desire to possess them forever.

The Holy Spirit's instruction will also allow the apostles in turn to teach others what Jesus taught them. After all, Jesus had commissioned them to go forth and "make disciples of all nations," baptizing them in the name of the Holy Trinity and teaching them to carry out everything He had commanded (see Matthew 28:19–20).

He Will Remind You of All That I Told You

As we saw in Chapter Two, the Spirit's work involves reminding us of all Jesus said. There are many hidden layers of meaning in the deeds and words of Our Lord; as the Holy Spirit leads us into all truth, He helps us fathom these deeper levels. He also enables us to see the connection between one event and another in Sacred Scripture.

For example, after the Resurrection the apostles were able to relate the words of the Old Testament—"Your king comes to you…riding on a donkey" (Zechariah 9:9, NRSV)—to the way the crowd received Jesus when he entered Jerusalem on a donkey on Palm Sunday (see John 12:12–15). John tells us: "His disciples did not understand this at first; but when Jesus was glorified, then they remembered that this had been written of him and had been done to him" (John 12:16).

Since Jesus was "glorified" by His resurrection, His ascension and His sending of the Holy Spirit—the three events form a unity of experience—this "remembering" occurs after the resurrection of Our Lord and after the coming of the Holy Spirit. Though the Holy Spirit is not directly mentioned in this Scripture verse, His work of reminding the apostles is assumed.

THIRD REFERENCE TO THE HOLY SPIRIT

"When the Paraclete comes, whom I shall send to you from the Father, the Spirit of truth who issues from the Father, he will be my witness. And you too will be witnesses, because you have been with me from the beginning" (John 15:26–27, NJB).

Whom I Myself Will Send from the Father

In the previous reference we saw the Holy Spirit as the Father's gift to us. Now we are reminded that He is also the gift of Jesus to us. In what way can we speak of the Holy Spirit as Jesus' gift to us?

First, Jesus merited this gift for us by His redemptive death. This is why Paul refers to the Holy Spirit as the "first fruits" (see Romans 8:23) and the "guarantee" (see 2 Corinthians 1:22) of our redemption. In other words, the Holy Spirit would not have been given to us unless Jesus merited Him as a gift for us from the Father by His redemptive death!

Second, Jesus sent the Spirit of truth to us as part of His glorification. As we have seen, His glorification consisted essentially of three things: His resurrection, through which He conquered the power of death and gave us the hope of eternal life; His ascension, through which He entered into His place of glory in heaven at the right hand of the Father; and His sending the Holy Spirit, who would perfect the growth of the Church Jesus founded, giving Jesus glory even on earth.

He Will Witness on My Behalf

Jesus would be glorified on earth precisely because the Spirit of truth would "witness" Jesus to His apostles and to all who would become His disciples through the end of time. He would witness in our minds and hearts—convince us and convict us—that Jesus is truly the Son of God and the Son of Mary and the only Savior of the world. He would also convince us of what Jesus has done for us.

Saint Paul gives numerous examples of this inner witness of the Holy Spirit, such as this passage from his powerful letter to the Christians at Rome:

> For all who are led by the Spirit of God are sons of God. For you did not receive the spirit of slavery to fall back into fear, but you have received the spirit of sonship. When we cry, "Abba! Father!" it is the Spirit himself bearing witness with our spirit that we are children of God, and if children, then heirs, heirs of God and fellow heirs with Christ, provided we suffer with him in order that we may also be glorified with him
>
> —ROMANS 8:14–17

You Must Bear Witness as Well

The Holy Spirit would also bear witness to Jesus externally by working various "signs and wonders" (see Acts 4:30; 5:12) through the hands of the apostles. The Acts of the Apostles contains many accounts of miracles that the apostles worked, including curing the sick (see 5:16; 28:8–9), healing the crippled (see 3:6–8; 14:10) and raising the dead (see 9:40). In addition, there were other deeds of great power that revealed the Holy Spirit at work, such as the judgment Peter passed on Ananias and Sapphira for their deceit (see 5:1–11) and the survival of Paul after a deadly snakebite (see 28:3–6). The people who saw these signs and wonders knew they confirmed the truth about Jesus.

The Holy Spirit also assisted those first disciples in witnessing to Jesus with their preaching. He gave them the courage to continue to speak "the word of God with boldness" (see Acts 4:31), especially in bearing witness to Jesus' resurrection. On Pentecost Peter proclaimed Jesus' resurrection, telling the crowd that the risen and now glorified Jesus had sent the Holy Spirit: "This Jesus God raised up, and of that we all are witnesses. Being therefore exalted at the right hand of God, and having received from the Father the promise of the Holy Spirit, he has poured out this which you see and hear" (Acts 2:32–33).

The Holy Spirit would move the apostles to give their supreme witness to Jesus by dying for their faith in Him. *Martyr,* in fact, is the Greek word for "witness"; martyrdom is the ultimate form of witness to Jesus.

FOURTH REFERENCE TO THE HOLY SPIRIT

Still, I am telling you the truth: It is for your own good that I am going, because unless I go, the Paraclete will not come to you; but if I go, I will send him to you. And when he comes, he will show the world how wrong it was about sin, and about who was in the right, and about judgment: about sin: in that they refuse to believe in me; about who was in the right: in that I am going to the Father and you will see me no more; about judgment: in that the prince of this world is already condemned. I still have many things to say to you but they would be too much for you to bear now. However, when the Spirit of truth comes he will lead you to the complete truth, since he will not be speaking of his own accord, but will say only what he has been told; and will reveal to you the things to come. He will glorify me, since all he reveals to you will be taken from what is mine.

—JOHN 16: 7–14, NJB

We have already examined why Jesus must go—so that the Holy Spirit, the other Paraclete, can come to continue and complete the mission of salvation and sanctification already begun by Jesus Himself. Jesus now reveals more about what the Spirit of truth will do when He comes. He will "show the world how wrong it was." "The world" here symbolizes all the forces opposed to Jesus and His Church. The Holy Spirit, the Advocate, like a prosecuting lawyer, will make His case against the world in regard to three things: sin, justice and condemnation.

He Will Prove the World Wrong About Sin

The great sin emphasized in the Gospel of John is the deliberate refusal of the people to believe that Jesus was who He claimed to be: the Messiah and the Son of God. Despite all His proofs, His miracles, His deeds of mercy and compassion, as well as His sublime teaching, many of the people, especially the leaders, hardened their hearts against Him. This sin—the unwillingness to believe—ultimately led them to reject Jesus.

When the Holy Spirit comes, He will make many of those who opposed Jesus and refused to accept Him realize the wrong—the sin—of this disbelief. This is a work He continues in the present.

He Will Prove the World Wrong About Justice

Most of the people rejected as blasphemous Jesus' claim to be the Son of the eternal Father. They viewed His humiliating death on the cross as vindication of their rejection. After all, they reasoned, if this were really God's Son, would His Father allow Him to die in such shame and suffering?

In reality, however, justice has now been accomplished: the Father raised Jesus, His Son, from the dead. Jesus triumphed still further by ascending to His place of glory in heaven at the right hand of His Father.

Through the Spirit of truth the apostles would preach this message boldly and confirm it with signs and wonders. This message and these miracles would condemn all those who said that Jesus had not come from the Father or that the Father did not support His Son and approve His sacrifice upon the cross. At the same time, this message would affirm those who accepted Jesus, strengthening their faith in His victory.

He Will Prove the World Wrong About Condemnation

The devil himself stirred the enemies of Jesus into rage and provoked them to seek His death upon the cross. Ironically, in God's plan, it was through the very act of Jesus' death that the devil would be defeated and his kingdom ultimately destroyed. By Jesus' death the judgment of condemnation has been passed upon the devil, the "prince of this world," and his kingdom has been overcome.

The Spirit of truth bears witness to this condemnation by the establishment of the kingdom of Christ in the Church. The kingdom of light has passed the judgment of condemnation upon the kingdom of darkness.

He Will Guide You to All Truth

The Spirit of truth will continue teaching the apostles where Jesus left off. He will not speak on His own or teach them a new or different doctrine. Rather He will build upon and intensify what Jesus has already taught.

Furthermore, the Spirit of truth will now use their experience of Jesus' death and resurrection—part of the hindsight vantage point we discussed in Chapter Two—as an essential element to complete their spiritual formation. The Spirit of truth will lead them to all truth. He will accomplish this by the infusion of His gifts, which will illuminate and expand their own limited human understanding.

We have now seen Jesus' description of the role of the Spirit of truth. This same Spirit continues to work in the Church today, just as He did among Jesus' apostles. The Spirit of truth is still leading the Church and each individual member of the Church into all truth, giving glory to Jesus and to the Father who sent Him.

CHAPTER 4

The Spirit at Work in the Early Church

WE CAN COMPARE THE GOVERNMENT and teaching authority of the Church to the essential elements of the human person. A human being consists of a body and a soul, a combination of something seen (or external) and something unseen (or interior). The material body, being external and therefore visible, is easily recognized. The soul, being spiritual and interior, is hidden and can only be recognized by the activities or results it produces in and through the body. Now, to be fully alive on earth, our soul and body must be united.[1] This is the way God made us.

Let's apply this image to the Roman Catholic Church. We see that God has established both an external agent and an interior agent in the governing and teaching offices of His Church. The external agent—the pope and bishops and those who assist them—is readily visible and therefore easily known and recognized. The interior agent—the Holy Spirit— is hidden from view.

Just as we can recognize the soul by its effects in the body, we recognize the Spirit by His activities in guiding the Church. He enlightens the members of the Church by helping them to understand Christ's teachings more fully, He protects these revealed truths from the falsehood of heresy, and He sees to it that these sacred doctrines are faithfully passed on and proclaimed from one generation of Catholic Christians to the next.

THE SPIRIT MOVES THE APOSTLES TO PREACH

In Scripture we see the external and internal agents working together to develop the teaching authority of the Church. The Acts of the Apostles, which records the first days and years of the Church's life, tells us, for example, that after the Holy Spirit came upon those first disciples at Pentecost, they began to proclaim "the mighty works of God" in many languages "as the Spirit gave them utterance" (Acts 2:11, 4). These disciples preached and taught externally what the Spirit, internally, inspired them to preach.

The Holy Spirit also strengthened and enlightened Peter when he was put on trial before the Jewish religious leaders in the Sanhedrin: "Then Peter, filled with the Holy Spirit, said to them, 'Rulers of the people and elders...'" (Acts 4:8). The Spirit strengthened all the early disciples, especially the apostles, with confidence to preach about Jesus without fear of persecution. He then confirmed their message by working many miracles through them. When Peter, for example, returned from speaking before the Sanhedrin, he joined the other disciples at prayer:

"And now, Lord, look at their threats, and grant to your servants to speak your word with all boldness, while you stretch out your hand to heal, and signs and wonders are performed through the name of your holy servant Jesus." When they had prayed, the place in which they were gathered together was shaken; and they were all filled with the Holy Spirit and spoke the word of God with boldness.... Now many signs and wonders were done among the people through the apostles.

—ACTS 4:29–31; 5:12, NRSV

THE HOLY SPIRIT AND THE FIRST GENTILE CONVERT

The Holy Spirit also guided the Church to a fuller understanding of the truth when He brought about the baptism of the first Gentile convert. The convert was Cornelius, a Roman centurion who, along with his household, is described as devout and God-fearing (Acts 10:2).[2] As a Jew, Peter was not to associate with Gentiles, but the Spirit led Peter to realize that now, in Christ, he must no longer consider "any man common or unclean" (see Acts 10:28). Moved by the Spirit, Saint Peter witnessed to Cornelius about Jesus and His mission of salvation. As a result, the first pope and vicar of Christ received this first Gentile convert into the faith and baptized him:

While Peter was still saying this, the Holy Spirit fell on all who heard the word. And the believers from among the circumcised [Christian converts from Judaism] who came with Peter were amazed, because the gift of the Holy Spirit had been poured out even on the Gentiles. For they heard them speaking in tongues and extolling God. Then Peter declared, "Can any one forbid water for baptizing these people who have received the Holy

Spirit just as we have?" And he commanded them to be baptized in the name of Jesus Christ.

—ACTS 10:44–48

The reception of the first Gentile convert into the Church was an enormous step forward in the Church's fuller understanding of her mission of universal salvation for all peoples, Jews and Gentiles alike. It was an important and early example of exactly how the Holy Spirit was guiding the Church "to all truth," as Jesus had promised.

THE HOLY SPIRIT AND THE MISSION OF PAUL

The conversion of Saul of Tarsus was another important step for the Church in her mission of working for the salvation of the world. In fact, so important was this event to the early Church that Saint Luke, the author of the Acts of the Apostles, recorded it three times (see Acts 9:1–30; 22:3–21; 26:4–23). Saint Paul was converted by Jesus Himself, who appeared to him in glory along the road to Damascus, transforming him from a relentless persecutor of the Church to her most zealous apostle. The Lord foretold that Saint Paul would be His chosen instrument (see Acts 9:15–16) to carry His name to the Gentiles, to kings as well as to the common people. He also foretold that Saint Paul would suffer much in the process.

Some time after his conversion, the Holy Spirit moved this great apostle of the Gentiles to go forth on the mission for which he had been chosen:

> Now in the church at Antioch there were prophets and teachers, Barnabas, Symeon who was called Niger, Lucius of Cyrene, Manaen a member of the court of Herod the tetrarch, and Saul. While they were worshipping

the Lord and fasting, the Holy Spirit said, "Set apart for me Barnabas and Saul for the work to which I have called them." Then after fasting and praying they laid their hands on them and sent them off.

—Acts 13:1–3

Throughout his missionary activity Saint Paul experienced the guidance, protection and consolation of the Holy Spirit.

THE HOLY SPIRIT DIRECTS THE FIRST COUNCIL OF THE CHURCH

Although all the disciples needed the help of the Holy Spirit, the leaders responsible for the doctrine and life of the early Church felt this need most of all. The experience of the Church in one of its first major crises illustrates how the Spirit of truth guided these leaders.

Some of the first generation of converts from Judaism to Christianity held that all potential Gentile converts first had to become Jewish. That is, they had to observe the rite of circumcision as well as the dietary laws and regulations of the Old Testament before they could become Christians. These "Judaizers," as they were sometimes called, were a constant source of trouble for Paul in his missionary work:

But some men came down from Judea and were teaching the brethren, "Unless you are circumcised according to the custom of Moses, you cannot be saved." And when Paul and Barnabas had no small dissension and debate with them, Paul and Barnabas and some of the others were appointed to go up to Jerusalem to the apostles and the elders about this question

—Acts 15:1–2

This council rejected the teaching that a Gentile had to be circumcised in order to become a Christian. The leaders then wrote a letter to the community of Christians at Antioch, chiefly Gentile converts, who had been disturbed by the false instruction. The letter expressed essential Church teaching in words that are significant for our understanding of the work of the Spirit:

> Forasmuch as we have heard that some of our number, without any instructions from us, have disturbed you with their talk and unsettled your minds, we have resolved unanimously to send to you our chosen representatives with our well-beloved Barnabas and Paul, who have devoted themselves to the cause of our Lord Jesus Christ. We are therefore sending Judas [Barsabbas] and Silas, who will themselves confirm this by word of mouth. It is the decision of the Holy Spirit, and our decision, to lay no further burden upon you beyond these essentials....
>
> —Acts 15:24–28, NEB

The key to this passage is the statement that this decision of the apostles and other Church leaders came from the direct guidance of the Holy Spirit and from their own authority as well, the interior and external forces in the teaching authority of the Church. The apostles, the visible factor, "bind and loose" with the authority Jesus gave them (see Matthew 16:18–19; 18:18). The Holy Spirit, the invisible factor, confirms the leaders' teaching by His infallible guidance.

THE HOLY SPIRIT IS STILL AT WORK IN THE CHURCH

Today it is necessary to stress once again that the work of the Holy Spirit is inseparable from the work of the authoritative leadership of the Church. These leaders form what is called the magisterium of the Church. The word *magisterium* is from the Latin word *magister*, which means "teacher." The magisterium of the Church, therefore, refers to her teaching office or authority. These leaders instruct us in the truths of divine revelation, namely the authentic doctrine and teaching of the Catholic Church.

This teaching authority resides in the pope himself, especially when he teaches *ex cathedra*—literally, "from the chair"—meaning when he officially exercises his teaching office. This authority also resides in the pope in union with the college of bishops, either gathered together for an ecumenical council or scattered throughout the world in their own dioceses. Priests and deacons as well as solidly orthodox theologians share in the teaching office of the Church as well.

If we separate the Holy Spirit from the magisterium, we inevitably fall into difficulty. For example, if we stress the guidance of the Holy Spirit to the neglect of authentic Church authority, we are in danger of forming an "inner light" Church that rejects the authority Jesus clearly gave to Peter and the apostles in favor of an interior enlightenment of the Holy Spirit. It is a simple next step for people to assume they have that "inner light" and that the principle of personal interpretation is the norm of truth.

It works this way: since "the Holy Spirit is guiding me," what I understand to be true is therefore true, at least for me. This approach produces sects and denominations that each claim to teach a "truth" the others do not have. An old Roman saying expresses it well: "As many persons as you have, that's how many opinions you will end up with!"

Referring back to our comparison with the human person, in this situation we would have a soul without a body, or the internal agent but not the external.

The opposite problem can occur if we isolate Church authority from the special guidance of the Holy Spirit. This would reduce the pope and the bishops to mere theologians offering "opinions" on moral or doctrinal questions. As a consequence, people would feel justified in dismissing what these leaders say on the grounds that their own opinions differ from those of Church leaders. And since, in this approach, the Holy Spirit is no longer viewed as guiding the teaching office in a unique way, safeguarding it from doctrinal error, the words of the magisterium would have no more value than anyone else's. Everyone would be entitled to offer his or her own theological guess!

Using the analogy of the human person again, we would have here a body without a soul. The external agent of the Church's teaching authority—namely, the pope and bishops—would be ineffective separated from the internal agent, the Holy Spirit. The result would be an endless series of opinions and theories leading inevitably to skepticism. Why? Because we would have no objective standard against which to measure our personal opinions, ideas and preferences. What would be the result? As a body without a soul is dead, so any teaching authority without authority to teach is useless!

The evidence is clear from sacred Scripture that the Lord Jesus sent the Spirit of truth to guide the teaching mission of the early Church. This has continued through the centuries and will continue until the Lord comes again at the end of time.

PART III

*The Spirit of Truth Raises Up
Different Witnesses of Truth*

CHAPTER 5

"Apostles, Prophets, Evangelists"

SAINT PAUL TELLS US that Christ set up certain offices of service for His mystical body, the Church. Those entrusted with these offices are responsible for guiding and protecting the Church, thereby ensuring that each member can grow to mature faith and proper knowledge of God. Paul lists five such "roles of service for the faithful": apostles, prophets, evangelists, pastors and teachers.

"And his [Christ's] gifts were that some should be apostles, some prophets, some evangelists, some pastors and teachers, for the equipment of the saints, for the work of ministry, for building up the body of Christ, until we all attain to the unity of the faith and of the knowledge of the Son of God, to mature manhood, to the measure of the stature of the fullness of Christ" (Ephesians 4:11–13). In this chapter we will look briefly at the offices of apostles, prophets and evangelists as they functioned in the early Church and as they still function today.

In apostolic times the official pastors and teachers of the Church also held the offices of apostle and evangelist. The apostles—as well as Saints Luke and Mark, the two evangelists who were not also apostles—were the first bishops of the Church. They were part of the magisterium.

Gradually others began to function as apostles and evangelists, a number of whom were not official pastors or teachers. Over time, in fact, these offices became more charismatic in nature. The Holy Spirit bestowed on individuals who were not necessarily part of the formal hierarchical structure the gifts necessary to accomplish certain tasks in the Church. Apostles, prophets and evangelists spoke God's word with striking power or acted in God's name in ways that had significant results for their listeners.

CHARISMATIC SERVICE

Apostles

The word *apostle* usually refers to one of the twelve apostles whom Jesus called during His public ministry. This is certainly the primary meaning of *apostle*. The twelve apostles were Jesus' closest companions and most privileged disciples. After His resurrection Jesus officially sent them forth to preach His gospel message of salvation to the whole world (see John 20:21; Acts 1:8).

Yet all three groups Paul first mentions—apostles, prophets, evangelists—are much broader in scope than we commonly understand them to be. In a secondary sense the title "apostle"—from a Greek word meaning "one who is sent"—applied to persons other than the twelve.[1] These seem to have had an itinerant ministry. They traveled from place to place, helping to establish the Church in various locations. They also seem to have assisted local Church authorities with the needs of the community, especially in those communities that were just getting organized.

Prophets

The word *prophet* comes from a Greek word meaning "one who speaks before others." It almost always indicates a person who communicates a divine message to others. Like the word *apostle*, *prophet* has both a narrow and a broad meaning.

In its more narrow or technical sense, the word refers to the prophets of the Old Testament. This clearly recognized group is often divided into various categories. Some, such as Elijah and Elisha, are considered "action prophets." They conveyed their messages in bold words and deeds. Then there are the "writing prophets." Of these Isaiah and Jeremiah have been designated "major" prophets, while Amos, Hosea, Malachi and others we call "minor" prophets. The works of the major prophets are longer and considered more significant than those of the minor prophets.

The New Testament applies the title "prophet" in a broader sense to individuals who speak an obviously inspired message or who share wisdom or understanding that can come only from someone who is truly of God. Interestingly, Jesus never called himself a prophet, though many others in the New Testament did, such as the Samaritan woman at the well (see John 4:19).

The First Letter to the Corinthians lists prophecy among the charismatic gifts (see 1 Corinthians 12:10). Those who spoke prophetically, like the broader group of apostles discussed above, were probably itinerant disciples who went from one local Christian community to another as the Spirit moved them. Their prophetic gift, exercised under the guidance of the Spirit of truth, generally included the ability to deliver an encouraging "word" or message to the community, to discern right from wrong regarding problematic issues and to call the community to faithfulness and reform.[2]

Evangelists

The title "evangelist" (from Greek, meaning "someone who brings good news") applies in its more restricted sense to the traditional four Evangelists—Saints Matthew, Mark, Luke and John—the writers of the four Gospels. Since these accounts of Jesus' life, death and resurrection contain His words and deeds, they are the Good News par excellence. It follows that the four Gospel writers are the evangelists par excellence!

The title also is given to charismatic itinerant preachers who went around to early Church communities and strengthened the faithful by their inspired preaching of the Word of God. The work of the famous preacher Apollos, mentioned in the Acts of the Apostles, is an outstanding example of this ministry:

> He was an eloquent man, well versed in the scriptures. He had been instructed in the way of the Lord; and being fervent in spirit, he spoke and taught accurately the things concerning Jesus.... He greatly helped those who through grace had believed, for he powerfully confuted the Jews in public, showing by the scriptures that the Christ was Jesus.
>
> —ACTS 18:24–25, 27–28

APOSTLES, PROPHETS AND EVANGELISTS IN THE CHURCH TODAY

The Lord Jesus continues to provide these three roles of service in His Church, though perhaps they are less obvious today as distinct ministries.

Apostles in Today's Church

Many in the Church carry out apostolic commitments as teachers, writers, administrators and other such roles in dioceses and parishes. Consecrated religious speak of their apostolates in nursing or in offering spiritual direction. The Holy Spirit is moving more and more laypeople to give of their time, talents and resources in caring for the poor and destitute in homeless shelters and soup kitchens. Others dedicate themselves to youth work or to pro-life issues.

The Spirit inspires these ministries, whether formal or informal, part-time or full-time. He calls forth individuals to be new apostles in the Church's field of labor.

Prophets in Today's Church

Either by word or deed, prophets proclaim a clear, significant message appropriate for the times. Mother Teresa of Calcutta, for example, was a truly prophetic person in the Church in the latter half of the twentieth century, calling people, by her example, to take action on behalf of the destitute.

Prophets are usually ahead of their times, inspired by the Spirit of truth to sense the direction in which the Church is moving or the great challenges ahead, before events prove them true. This can cause them a great deal of suffering, especially when their contemporaries misunderstand them. But when the Church lacks a sufficient number of prophetic people, lethargy and stagnation result. People naturally gravitate toward maintaining the status quo rather than embracing a vibrant, Spirit-filled attitude of growth and effort to extend the kingdom of God.

Evangelists in Today's Church

Evangelization in the Church must continue until the end of time, for Jesus has commanded us to preach the Good News to all creation (see Mark 16:15). Jesus calls all members of the Church, from the pope and bishops to the newly baptized, to preach about Him and witness Him to others by words and deeds. Sometimes He gives the Church outstanding evangelizers such as the late Pope John Paul II and Archbishop Fulton Sheen. Their words have had an obvious anointing of the Holy Spirit, a certain power given by the Spirit of truth to penetrate minds and hearts. But all of us must use our natural gifts and talents as well as the supernatural graces God has given us to carry on the Church's ministry of evangelization.

This is the challenge John Paul II set before the Church with his summons to a "new evangelization" in the world: "I sense that the moment has come to commit all of the Church's energies to a new evangelization and to the mission *ad gentes*. No believer in Christ, no institution of the Church can avoid this supreme duty: to proclaim Christ to all peoples."[3]

This challenge sounds like that of a pope of old issuing a call for a crusade, a holy war. This crusade, however, will not be fought with weapons of violence and destruction but with the weapons of holiness and truth, justice and love. It will be accomplished in witness to the living, risen Savior of the world and the eternal Father who sent Him "for us men and for our salvation," as we proclaim in the Nicene Creed.

In the pope's view the Holy Spirit will be the one who will guide and coordinate this great work of the new evangelization. In his talks and writings the Holy Father referred to the Holy Spirit as "the active Agent of the Church's evangelizing mission"[4] and "the principal Agent of the new evangelization."[5]

Let us pray that our heavenly Father will send the Spirit of truth upon the Church again, as He did at that first Pentecost. Let us pray that He will move all of us to proclaim in our words and deeds—in fact, to cry out with our lives—the Good News of salvation: Christ has died, alleluia! Christ has risen, alleluia! Christ will come again, alleluia!

THE SPIRIT'S CHARISMATIC GIFTS

This discussion of apostles, evangelists and prophets has touched on the subject of charismatic gifts. Saint Paul teaches us how the Holy Spirit distributes and uses His charismatic gifts for the welfare of the whole Church. Let us look at three points the Apostle to the Gentiles makes in his First Letter to the Corinthians.

There Is a Variety of Gifts

First he says: "There are varieties of gifts, but the same Spirit" (1 Corinthians 12:4). Jesus referred to the Holy Spirit as "the gift of God" (John 4:10) because the Father gives Him to us through the Son, as the special gift or fruit of the Son's redemptive mission. But the Holy Spirit in turn is a giver of gifts. The Church distinguishes two types of His gifts, based on Sacred Scripture.

In the Book of Isaiah, we find reference to the Spirit's "sevenfold" or "sanctifying" gifts: wisdom, understanding, knowledge, counsel, fortitude, piety and fear of the Lord (see Isaiah 11:2–3).[6] The Spirit gives us these gifts at the moment of our baptism, when we receive our new life in Christ by "water and the Spirit" (John 3:5). All these gifts are present in us as long as we are in the state of grace. They are meant for our personal sanctification and growth in virtue. They make us more receptive to the inspirations of the Holy Spirit and thus help us do good and avoid evil. These gifts grow and develop in us as we mature in our spiritual life.

There Are Gifts for the Whole Church

Saint Paul makes a second point about the Holy Spirit's gifts. He says, "To each is given the manifestation of the Spirit for the common good" (1 Corinthians 12:7). This leads us to consider the second type of gifts the Holy Spirit gives us— namely, the charismatic gifts. The "common good" Saint Paul is referring to is the growth and development of the Church as a whole. Whereas the sanctifying gifts assist the spiritual growth of individuals, the charismatic gifts assist the well-being of the whole mystical body of Christ.

Saint Paul lists these gifts in a few places in his writings.[7] His lists, though, are not exhaustive; the Church recognizes many more charismatic gifts. One only has to think of someone like Saint Padre Pio and his gifts of bilocation, fragrance and probably the stigmata. As we have seen earlier, Saint Paul told the Ephesians that God gives His gifts and roles of service to build up the body of Christ till it reaches its full perfection. These gifts do not of themselves make the individuals who possess them holy, nor are they necessarily an absolute sign of great holiness.[8]

The Spirit Gives His Gifts as He Chooses

The third point Saint Paul makes is that the Holy Spirit bestows His charismatic gifts on those whom He chooses and for His own purposes: "All these [gifts] are inspired by one and the same Spirit, who apportions to each one individually as he wills" (1 Corinthians 12:11). The Holy Spirit is the "spiritual director" of the Church. He freely gives His gifts to certain individuals, whom He wishes to carry out His purposes in and for the mystical body.[9] This is why one person may be called to be an apostle, another an evangelist and still another a prophet. Someone may receive two or even all three of these calls.

So it is with the remainder of the charisms. Because different individuals possess different charismatic gifts, the Church as a whole will possess a fullness of the Spirit's gifts. Thus, when needs arise within the community, one or another person will possess the gifts required to meet those needs.

EXAMPLES OF CHARISMATIC GIFTS AT WORK IN THE CHURCH

Someone may possess the gift of "wisdom in discourse." This is a special ability to teach the truths of the Catholic faith with clarity and facility, both to Catholics who are well educated in their faith as well as to those who have received only a little or even no previous religious instruction.

The gift to "distinguish between spirits" allows a person to discern whether something is coming from the Holy Spirit, the devil or an individual's own human spirit. This is important because the devil tries to come as an "angel of light" (2 Corinthians 11:14), to lead us into evil under the appearance of good.

"Miraculous powers" is another charismatic gift. Someone with this gift is able to edify both believers and non-believers with marvelous signs and wonders. Such miracles can strengthen the faith of those who believe and assist others to be disposed to receive the gift of faith.

All the charismatic gifts are necessary, and that is why the Holy Spirit distributes them as He wills. In the Church community we must all work together in love for God and for one another, in order to bring the mystical body of Christ to its fullness. As Saint Paul also wrote, each has his or her gift. Just as the human body needs ears as well as eyes and feet as well as hands, so everyone's gifts are important (see 1 Corinthians 12).

When all the members of the Church with their particular gifts work together, the unity of the Church is more deeply expressed, and her work bears more abundant fruit. The Holy Spirit directs this great work!

PART IV

The Spirit of Truth Guides Those in Pastoral Office

CHAPTER 6

The Spirit of Truth and the Role of Pastors in the Church

SAINT PAUL LISTS "PASTOR" as a role of service within the Church community (see Ephesians 4:11). *Pastor* means "shepherd" in Latin. The image of the shepherd with his sheep is one of the oldest and most beloved in Scripture. Adam and Eve's second son, Abel, for example, is described as a "keeper of sheep" (Genesis 4:2). Jacob, the great patriarch, was a shepherd, as was David when he was anointed to succeed King Saul as king of Israel (see 1 Samuel 16:10–13). Focusing on the rich biblical imagery of shepherds can help us better appreciate the role of pastor.

THE LORD IS SHEPHERD OF HIS PEOPLE

It was common among pagan nations in the ancient Near East to regard both their kings and their gods as shepherds. The king Hammurabi and the god Shamash, for example, were both addressed as shepherds. It is not surprising, then, that the Jews, a pastoral people, considered God Himself their

> Know that the Lord is God!
> It is he that made us, and we are
> his;
> we are his people, and the sheep
> of his pasture.
>
> —PSALM 100:3

> The Lord is my shepherd, I
> shall not want.
> He makes me lie down in
> green pastures;
> he leads me beside still waters;
> he restores my soul.
> He leads me in right paths
> for his name's sake.
> Even though I walk through the
> darkest valley,
> I fear no evil;
> for you are with me;
> your rod and your staff—
> they comfort me.
>
> —PSALM 23:1–4, NRSV

Ezekiel the prophet speaks of the coming Messiah in terms of a kindly shepherd. He will not only lead his sheep to water and rest, he will also gather the strays and bind up the wounds of the injured. Jesus, in fact, identifies Himself as the "Good Shepherd" and is represented as such in the earliest Christian art. His mission is described as being exclusively to "the lost sheep of the house of Israel" (Matthew 10:6; 15:24). He is the compassionate shepherd who leaves the ninety-nine sheep to go in search of the one lost sheep and then rejoices when He finds it (see Luke 15:4–7); He is the fearless shepherd willing to face thieves and wolves who attack the flock; He is the loving shepherd willing to lay down His life for His sheep (see John 10:11–15).

The Demanding Life of a Shepherd

The life of a shepherd was fraught with danger. On one occasion, for example, young King David related that he had killed a lion and bear with his own hands when they attacked the flock he was watching over (see 1 Samuel 17:34–37). Needless to say, the role required dedication and sacrifice:

> The type of pasture available in biblical regions imposes upon the shepherd the necessity of the nomadic life; he must travel with his flock from one pasture to another as the seasons change. Sheep find grass even where there appears to be little and need to be watered only once daily; but they must be led to both pasture and water. The shepherd also leads them to shelter in inclement weather and defends them against beasts of prey and bandits.[1]

Through his constant presence and wholehearted service to his sheep, the shepherd established a close bond with each of them, much like the proverbial relationship of a boy with his dog.

> The shepherd establishes a remarkable rapport with his flock; they recognize his voice and distinguish it from others and learn to obey commands given by voice. They seem to have perfect confidence in their shepherd and follow him wherever he leads. The shepherd keeps the flock together, going to great trouble to search out

strayed sheep, knowing that the flock will docilely remain together until he returns.[2]

A PASTOR IS A SHEPHERD OF SOULS

There are two important parallels that we can draw between the experience of shepherds and the role of pastors in the Church. The first is that the life of a pastor requires a dedication that is both constant and sacrificial; the role cannot be taken lightly or be considered a trivial task. Here is how Saint Peter described the attitude of a true pastor of the Church:

> So I exhort the elders among you, as a fellow elder and a witness of the sufferings of Christ as well as a partaker in the glory that is to be revealed. Tend the flock of God that is your charge, not by constraint but willingly, not for shameful gain but eagerly, not as domineering over those in your charge but being examples to the flock. And when the chief Shepherd is manifested you will obtain the unfading crown of glory.
>
> —1 PETER 5:1–4

We have seen how the needs of the flock in a real sense determined the lifestyle of the shepherd. A true shepherd—as opposed to a "hireling"—had to be willing to forego his own plans and satisfactions in order to meet the needs of the flock. The pastor of Christ's flock, like the shepherd with his sheep, must spend himself in the service of his people regardless of the cost.

The second parallel is that a true pastor must have a genuine personal love and concern for the flock entrusted to his care. Just as the shepherd knows each of his sheep by name, the pastor should learn to recognize the people in his congregation as far as possible. He should acquaint himself with their general and, wherever possible, individual needs. He should be concerned for the young and the aged, the-healthy as well as the sick and the handicapped, the learned and the simple, the rich and the poor.

The shepherd in Israel typically walks at the front of his flock (see John 10:4); so the true pastor should inspire and lead his community by good example, by practicing what he preaches. If he adds charity and compassion to sound teaching, he will help his congregation be of one mind and heart (see Acts 4:32), expressing the unity of the Church. The pastor must likewise be concerned with those who no longer practice their Catholic faith, seeking them out as a shepherd searches for the lost sheep (see Luke 15:4–7).

ORDAINED FOR SERVICE, HOLINESS, FAITHFULNESS

There are three essential attitudes that should characterize the shepherds of the Church if they are to lead God's people to holiness of life.

Service

Pastors, by their sacred orders, must imitate Jesus in a special way, since they uniquely share His eternal priesthood. Jesus frequently stressed to His apostles that He had come to serve and not to be served (see Matthew 20:28; Mark 10:45; Luke 22:27). He wanted His apostles to have this same attitude. In order to impress this on them, when He gave them the power of His priesthood at the Last Supper, He first washed their feet. This was the work of slaves. By His actions Jesus made the point that the apostles were not to exercise their priestly authority by force or domination, as worldly rulers might do (see Luke 22:25–26). Rather, their role was to be one of loving service to God and to His people, who after all are simply their brothers and sisters in Christ.

Holiness

The bishop tells the new priests he ordains, "Know what you are doing, and imitate the mystery you celebrate: model your life on the mystery of the Lord's cross."[3] In carrying out their roles of service arising from the sacrament of holy orders, pastors must strive for a holiness befitting their share in the ministerial priesthood of Jesus. They must become holy, since they serve the all-holy Lord.

Faithfulness

Pastors must also be trustworthy or faithful. Saint Paul tells us: "This is how one should regard us, as servants of Christ and stewards of the mysteries of God. Moreover it is required of stewards that they be found trustworthy" (1 Corinthians 4:1–2).

A pastor is trustworthy when he faithfully carries out his priestly duties, motivated by love for the Lord and his brothers and sisters in Christ. A trustworthy pastor has a genuine sense of responsibility for the spiritual and even temporal welfare of those placed in his charge. He renders his service faithfully, knowing that someday he must give an account of his pastoral stewardship—his shepherding—to Jesus, the eternal Shepherd.

This is a sobering thought. In his sermon "On Pastors," the fourth-century bishop Saint Augustine of Hippo, one of the greatest bishops in Church history, described his thoughts about shepherding the flock of believers committed to his care:

> You have often learned that all our hope is in Christ and that he is our true glory and our salvation. You are members of the flock of the Good Shepherd, who watches over Israel and nourishes his people. Yet there are shepherds who want to have the title of shepherd without wanting to fulfill a pastor's duties; let us then recall what God says to His shepherds through the prophet [Ezekiel]. You must listen attentively; I must listen with fear and trembling…
>
> I must distinguish carefully between two aspects of the role the Lord has given me, a role that demands a vigorous accountability, a role based on the Lord's greatness rather than on my own merit. The first aspect is that I am a Christian; the second, that I am a leader. I am a Christian for my own sake, whereas I am a leader for your sake; the fact that I am a Christian is to my own advantage, but I am a leader to your advantage. Many persons come to God as Christians but not as leaders. Perhaps they travel by an easier road and are less hindered since they bear a lighter burden. In addition to the fact that I am a Christian and must give God an account of my life, I as a leader must give Him an account of my stewardship as well.[4]

JESUS GIVES THE HOLY SPIRIT TO THE PASTORS OF HIS CHURCH

When our risen Lord had completed His mission of redemption and was about to ascend to His place of glory at the right hand of His heavenly Father, He told His apostles that He was sending them on a mission to Jerusalem, Judea, Samaria and even to the very ends of the earth (see Acts 1:8). They were to be His witnesses, proclaiming the good news about Him everywhere and carrying on His threefold mission of sanctifying, governing and teaching His people.

In preparing them for this task, Jesus emphasized: "Wait for the promise of the Father.... You shall be baptized with the Holy Spirit.... You shall receive power when the Holy Spirit has come upon you" (Acts 1:4, 5, 8).

The apostles were not to go until the Spirit of truth had come. Peter and the apostles had to have the power of the Holy Spirit, the true Sanctifier. So it is now for the pope and the bishops as their successors.

It is the Holy Spirit's work to guide the mission of the Church, especially in and through her pastors. To be dedicated and zealous in their vocations and to effectively carry out their mission of sanctifying others, pastors first need to experience the sanctifying power of the Holy Spirit in their own lives. They need the guidance and counsel of the Holy Spirit before they can teach with the authority of Christ. They need the Spirit of truth to lead them into all truth and bring to mind all that Jesus has taught before they in turn can govern the flock of Christ. Indeed, the threefold mission of Jesus cannot be carried on apart from the Paraclete, who has come to complete the work Jesus began.

A SHARE IN THE THREEFOLD MESSIANIC MISSION OF JESUS

Pastors—the pope, bishops, priests and deacons—share in the threefold mission that Jesus, as the Christ or the Anointed

One, carried out in His own life: the mission of priest, king and prophet.

> The word "Christ" comes from the Greek translation of the Hebrew *Messiah*, which means "anointed." It became the name proper to Jesus only because he accomplished perfectly the divine mission that "Christ" signifies. In effect, in Israel those consecrated to God for a mission that he gave were anointed in his name. This was the case for kings, for priests and, in rare instances, for prophets. This had to be the case all the more so for the Messiah whom God would send to inaugurate his kingdom definitively. It was necessary that the Messiah be anointed by the Spirit of the Lord at once as king and priest, and also as prophet. Jesus fulfilled the messianic hope of Israel in his threefold office of priest, prophet, and king. (*Catechism of the Catholic Church*, #436)

We have emphasized the role our pastors—our shepherds— play in teaching and safeguarding all that God has revealed through the Spirit of truth.[5] This role reflects their sharing in the prophetic office of Jesus. In the following chapters we will look at all three aspects of Jesus' messianic mission—His priestly, kingly and prophetic offices—and further examine how the shepherds of the Church have a special share in all of these. 🕊

CHAPTER 7

Pastors and the Priestly Office of Jesus

THE PRIESTLY OFFICE OF JESUS refers to His being, as man, the perfect mediator between the Trinity and the human race. This is precisely what a priest is: a mediator between God and humanity. Since Jesus alone is both God and man, He as man is our eternal high priest. He perfectly represents His heavenly Father and the Father's will to us, while representing all of us and all our concerns to His heavenly Father.

Jesus' sanctifying mission on our behalf flows from His priestly office. He exercises this mission in many ways: as the head of His mystical body, the Church, He leads us in our worship of the most holy Trinity; He offers constant intercessory prayer before the Trinity for all our needs, spiritual and temporal (see Hebrews 7:25); He dispenses the Father's love and mercy to us through the sacraments, above all through the sacrifice of the Mass, in which He renews in an unbloody manner His offering of Himself for us upon the cross at Calvary, a victim of love and mercy.

PASTORS SHARE UNIQUELY IN JESUS' PRIESTLY OFFICE

Those whom Jesus established to shepherd His Church share uniquely in His priestly mission through the sacrament of holy orders. This includes, primarily, the pope and the bishops in union with him, as successors of Saint Peter and the apostles. It also includes priests who, by virtue of ordination, are coworkers of the bishops. Deacons participate but only in roles of service. Each shares according to the specific "ordination" he has received.[1]

Although the laity also share in the priestly mission of Jesus through the sacrament of baptism (as we shall see in a later chapter), pastors—bishops and priests—share in the priestly mission of Jesus in a radically different and unique way through the sacrament of holy orders. This is not merely a difference in degree of intensity or a difference of life situation. There is an essential and far-reaching difference between the universal priesthood of the faithful, shared by all the baptized, and the ministerial priesthood, shared only by those men who are ordained.

As the *Catechism of the Catholic Church* states:

> The ministerial or hierarchical priesthood of bishops and priests, and the common priesthood of all the faithful participate, "each in its own proper way, in the one priesthood of Christ." While being "ordered one to another," they differ essentially. In what sense? While the common priesthood of the faithful is exercised by the unfolding of baptismal grace—a life of faith, hope, and charity, a life according to the Spirit—the ministerial priesthood is at the service of the common priesthood. It is directed at the unfolding of the baptismal grace of all

Christians. The ministerial priesthood is a means by which Christ unceasingly builds up and leads his Church. For this reason it is transmitted by its own sacrament, the sacrament of Holy Orders. (#1547)

This share in Jesus' threefold mission through holy orders is so profound that it enables those men who are ordained to speak and act in the person of Jesus Himself[2]: "In the ecclesial service of the ordained minister, it is Christ himself who is present to his Church as Head of his Body, Shepherd of his flock, high priest of the redemptive sacrifice, Teacher of Truth. This is what the Church means by saying that the priest, by virtue of the sacrament of Holy Orders, acts 'in persona Christi Capitis' ['in the person of Christ the Head']" (*CCC*, #1548).

Let's look at how bishops and priests share in Jesus' priestly office or sanctifying mission for the Church.

BISHOPS

A bishop possesses the fullness of the ministerial priesthood of Jesus; therefore bishops, first and foremost, share in the priestly office of Jesus. The Second Vatican Council's Constitution on the Church teaches that "the fullness of the sacrament of Orders is conferred by episcopal consecration, that fullness...which...is called the high priesthood, the acme of the sacred ministry...Episcopal consecration confers...the office of sanctifying."[3] As to how the bishop carries out his priestly or sanctifying role, the Constitution on the Sacred Liturgy from Vatican II states two important principles.

THE BISHOP LEADS HIS DIOCESE IN PRAYER
AND WORSHIP

First, it is the bishop who presides when his people assemble, especially for the celebration of the holy sacrifice of the Mass and of the sacraments. He represents Christ to his flock as he leads his people in prayer and worship. Vatican II's Constitution on the Liturgy states:

> The bishop is to be considered as the high priest of his flock from whom the life in Christ of His faithful is in some way derived and upon whom it in some way depends. Therefore all should hold in greatest esteem the liturgical life of the diocese centered around the bishop, especially in his cathedral church. They must be convinced that the principal manifestation of the Church consists in the full, active participation of all God's holy people in the same liturgical celebrations, especially in the same Eucharist, in one prayer, at one altar, at which the bishop presides, surrounded by his college of priests and by his ministers. (41)

The liturgical prayer life of a diocese, therefore, centers around its bishop. The earthly liturgy with the faithful gathered in worship and praise around the bishop, the high priest of the diocese, resembles, though imperfectly, the glorious heavenly liturgy, with all the saints gathered in worship and praise around Jesus, the eternal High Priest. Even when the bishop cannot be present at a liturgical celebration of his people, his primacy of place in leading the worship of his diocese is remembered, as when a priest mentions the names of both the pope and the local diocesan bishop during the Eucharistic Prayer.

Every bishop, then, should be a man of prayer, open to the Holy Spirit and attentive to His inspirations. First he should lead his people by example, and then he should guide them by his teaching and directives—like Jesus Himself, who "[first] did and [then] taught" (see Acts 1:1, NRSV). The bishop should foster the piety and devotion of the faithful and encourage their frequent participation in the sacraments.

The Bishop Regulates the Sacred Liturgy in His Diocese

In addition to presiding over the liturgical celebrations in his diocese, the bishop is to see that others—priests and various liturgical ministers—carry out the liturgy properly. The Constitution on the Sacred Liturgy says that the "regulation of the sacred liturgy depends solely on the authority of the Church, that is, on the Apostolic See, and, as laws may determine, on the bishop" (22).

The Council's Constitution on the Church states further that the bishop's authority to regulate the liturgy in his diocese is seen in his authority over the various sacraments as they are carried out in his diocese.

> The bishop, invested with the fullness of the sacrament of orders, is "the steward of the graces of the supreme priesthood," above all in the Eucharist, which he himself offers, or ensures that it is offered, from which the Church ever derives its life and on which it thrives…. Moreover, every legitimate celebration of the Eucharist is regulated by the bishop…. Through the sacraments, the frequent and fruitful distribution of which they regulate by their authority, [the bishops] sanctify the faithful. They control the conferring of Baptism, through which a sharing in the [common or universal] priesthood of Christ is granted.

> They are the original ministers of Confirmation; it is they who confer sacred Orders and regulate the discipline of Penance, and who diligently exhort and instruct their flocks to take the part that is theirs, in a spirit of faith and reverence, in the liturgy and above all in the holy sacrifice of the Mass. (26)

The bishop must be the first in his diocese to observe the decrees of the Holy See in regard to the sacred liturgy. This would include such matters as using only approved rituals, translations of liturgical texts and the like. He leads by example.

The bishop then must see that his priests and other ministers do the same. He must guard against abuses as well as distortions of sound spirituality.[4] When such distortions and abuses creep in, the bishop must work to remove them by a blend of truth, kindness, firmness, patience, love and, when necessary, the disciplinary force of the authority of his office. The proper functioning of the diocese as well as the spiritual welfare of the faithful demand the urgent correction of those abuses that obviously offend and even scandalize the people of God.

Let us conclude our reflections on the bishop's share in the priestly office of Jesus with a statement from the Church's canon law:

> Since the diocesan bishop is mindful of his obligation to show an example of holiness in charity, humility, and simplicity of life, he is to strive to promote in every way the holiness of the Christian faithful according to the proper vocation of each. Since he is the principal dispenser of the mysteries of God, he is to endeavor constantly that the Christian faithful entrusted to his care

grow in grace through the celebration of the sacraments and that they understand and live the paschal mystery. (canon 387)

PRIESTS

Priests also share in the ministerial priesthood of Jesus but in a way subordinate to and dependent upon the bishop. The Second Vatican Council's Constitution on the Church calls priests "prudent cooperators" of the bishops as well as a "support and mouthpiece" for them (28):

> In each local assembly of the faithful [priests] represent in a certain sense the bishop, with whom they are associated in all trust and generosity; in part they take upon themselves his duties and solicitude and in their daily toils discharge them. Those who, under the authority of the bishop, sanctify and govern the portion of the Lord's flock assigned to them render the universal Church visible in their locality and contribute efficaciously towards building up the whole [mystical] body of Christ. (28)

This same document lists the important duties of priests derived from their sacerdotal—priestly— ordination. It states that priests are consecrated to celebrate the divine worship, preeminently in offering the holy sacrifice of the Mass; to preach the gospel by announcing the Word of God and to carry out in an eminent degree a ministry of reconciliation in the confessional for those moved to sorrow for their sins and a ministry of comfort for those stricken with sickness (see *Lumen gentium,* 28).

Priests further assist in the sanctifying mission of Jesus by the good example of Christian virtue and priestly dedication in their personal lives, by intercessory prayer for the faithful and by leading the faithful in prayer and the ways of prayer. In addition, they assist the faithful through instruction and spiritual direction as well as with words of counsel in times of doubt, encouragement in times of fear and consolation in the face of sorrow and despair.

DEACONS

The deacons constitute the third level of the hierarchy. They receive a sacramental act of ordination that does not confer the priesthood but rather a ministry for the Church. Deacons are "intended to help and serve" the bishops and the priests (*CCC*, #1554).

> For, strengthened by sacramental grace [deacons] are dedicated to the People of God, in conjunction with the bishop and his body of priests, in the service of the liturgy, of the Gospel and of works of charity. It pertains to the office of a deacon, insofar as it may be assigned to him by the competent authority, to administer Baptism solemnly, to be custodian and distributor of the Eucharist, in the name of the Church, to assist at and bless marriages, to bring Viaticum to the dying, to read the sacred scriptures to the faithful, to instruct and exhort the people, to preside over the worship and the prayer of the faithful, to administer sacramentals, and to officiate at funeral and burial services. (*Lumen gentium*, 29)

THE ROLE OF THE HOLY SPIRIT IN THE PRIESTLY LIFE AND MINISTRY OF PASTORS

The Holy Spirit plays a central role in the lives and ministries of those who share the ministerial priesthood of Jesus. This was clearly brought home to me at my own ordination at the hands of Fulton Sheen, then bishop of Rochester, New York. After the ceremony he told me, "Today you have received the power of the Holy Spirit!" As the years have gone by, these words have stuck with me, making me increasingly aware of the presence and activity of the Holy Spirit in my priestly life and ministry.

The Holy Spirit in the Life of a Priest

A priest cannot live his vocation to the full unless the Holy Spirit is active in his life and ministry. It is the Holy Spirit who helps him cry out: "Abba,...Father" (Romans 8:15; Galatians 4:6). It is the Spirit who will sustain a priest in the faithful life of prayer so essential to being a good priest. In moments when he prays, as well as when he meditatively reflects on Sacred Scripture, he feels the power of the Word of God. This is because Scripture is inspired, it is breathed through-and-through with the life-giving breath of the Holy Spirit who is the very breath of God. The Spirit of truth makes the Word of God come alive for the priest and in him. It thus becomes a living, saving and sanctifying Word that he can share effectively with God's people.

The Holy Spirit is truly the sanctifier of men chosen by God the Father and called by Jesus to share in the sacrament of holy orders. Bishops and priests must be holy according to the dignity of their sacramental order. Since they are to speak and act "in the person of Christ," they must resemble Him by the holiness of their own lives, reproducing in their thoughts, words and deeds the virtues they see in Jesus. Accordingly the Holy Spirit, like a great sculptor of clay, molds their minds and hearts to so resemble Jesus that every bishop and priest should be able to say with Paul: "It is no longer I who live, but Christ who lives in me; and the life I now live in the flesh I live by faith in the Son of God, who loved me and gave himself for me" (Galatians 2:20).

The ordained must respond to the promptings of the Holy Spirit. They must do their part faithfully. As Saint Augustine put it, "While he made you without you, he does not justify you without you!"[5] Through heartfelt daily prayer, through appropriate mortification and self-denial and through a consistent, genuine effort to practice the virtues—especially charity, meekness, humility, kindness, chastity and modesty—the life of a priest is gradually transformed until he becomes truly an *alter Christus*, another Christ!

The Holy Spirit in the Ministry of Pastors

Bishops and priests should be conscious of the Holy Spirit as they minister, invoking His power continually. They call on Him particularly during sacramental moments. When they consecrate the bread and wine at Mass, for example, they invoke the Holy Spirit. Just before the consecration they extend their hands over the gifts of bread and wine and call down the Holy Spirit upon the gifts, such as in Eucharistic Prayer III: "And so, Father, we bring you these gifts. We ask you to make them holy by the power of your Spirit, that they may become the Body and Blood of your Son, Our Lord Jesus Christ, at whose command we celebrate this Eucharist."

They also call upon the power of the Holy Spirit in the sacrament of reconciliation. The formula of absolution from sins states in part: "God, the Father of mercies, through the death and resurrection of His Son, has reconciled the world to Himself and sent the Holy Spirit among us for the forgiveness of sins."[6]

When bishops and priests confer the sacrament of baptism, they beget new life in Christ by means of "water and the Spirit" (see John 3:5). When bishops or priests confirm,[7] they use the formula: "Receive the seal of the Holy Spirit, the gift of the Father." They confer the Holy Spirit in the sacrament of confirmation in such a way as to complete baptism, making the recipient of confirmation a mature, adult Christian and a witness of Christ in his or her life. In holy orders bishops confer the power of the Holy Spirit to those being ordained as bishops, priests or deacons.

THE EFFECTS OF HOLINESS ON A PRIEST'S MINISTRY

It is important to state clearly that the validity of the sacramental ministry of a priest does not depend on his personal holiness. As long as he is validly ordained and carries out the rites of the sacraments correctly (for example, he offers Mass or absolves a penitent according to the proper form), the sacrament is validly given. The recipient would receive the effects and graces of the sacrament even if the priest were in the state of mortal sin.[8] As Saint Augustine said, when Peter baptizes, it is Christ who baptizes; when Paul baptizes, it is Christ who baptizes; even when Judas baptizes, it is still Christ who baptizes.[9]

The Church clarified this teaching in opposition to the Donatist heresy, which arose during the Roman persecutions of the Church in the fourth century. The Donatists believed that sacraments conferred by apostate priests—priests who had renounced their faith under persecution—or priests guilty of heresy or serious personal sin were invalid. The Donatists said that such ministers were deprived of the Holy Spirit and His grace and so were incapable of transmitting grace to others through the sacraments. Despite decisions from Rome and from a council at Arles that condemned them, the Donatists refused to abandon their errors and organized their own schismatic church.

Saint Augustine, the "Doctor of Grace," kindly but thoroughly refuted their arguments at a council at Carthage. He pointed out that the Church on earth was not a society of saints, as the Donatists held, but a mixed body of good and bad clergy and laity. He also said that the sacraments drew their efficacy from Christ, who acts in all the sacraments, not from their human ministers. As a result, the majority of Donatists returned to the Church.

If the sacraments were dependent on the worthiness of their human ministers, we would be faced with an intolerable situation. If we are unsure the priest offering Mass is in a state of grace, for example, we might wonder if we are attending a valid Mass and if we are receiving the Body and Blood of the Lord in the Eucharist or just a wafer of bread. The same uncertainty would be present with other sacraments. The Lord offsets this possibility by providing that the priest always acts in His person every time he administers the sacrament validly.

This is not to say that the personal holiness of the priest is unimportant. Far from it; it has a far-reaching effect! First of all, a holy priest will always administer the sacraments while in the state of sanctifying grace. In this way he guards against any unworthy, sacrilegious fulfillment of his sacred duties.

Likewise he will be careful not to fall into patterns of neglect (not caring how he says Mass or carries out the sacramental rites) or lukewarmness (lacking a sincere motivation of love) or routine (merely going through the motions).

Furthermore, if a priest's heart is Christlike, he will carry out the sacred mysteries of the Mass and the sacraments with a genuine and unaffected devotion and reverence. With eyes of faith, he will never forget that he is touching what is sacred. Filled with the love of Jesus poured into his heart by the Holy Spirit, he will offer dedicated service to God and to His People. Such a disposition of holiness will have a powerful impact on the faithful. They will be genuinely edified, and this edification, in turn, will stir them to attend Mass and receive Holy Communion or any other sacrament with a more lively faith and genuine love of God. This increases their receptivity to the effects of the sacraments.

There is a traditional saying in the Catholic Church:

> If you have saintly priests, you will have holy people;
> If you have holy priests, you will have good people;
> If you have good priests, you will have mediocre people;
> If you have mediocre priests, you will have bad people;
> If you have bad priests, you will have beasts for people!

The Holy Spirit, by His inspirations and gifts, moves priests to live holy and dedicated lives. He fills them with joy in being priests and in carrying out their priestly duties. He enkindles in their hearts, in response to the love of Jesus crucified, a great desire for the salvation of souls. With Saint John Bosco zealous priests cry, "Give me souls and take all the rest!"[10] This joy and zeal can give priests an incredible sense of fulfillment, making them even more zealous for the things of God.

The Priesthood Under Attack

There is no doubt that the Roman Catholic priesthood is under deliberate attack today by many powerful and influential people in the secular world. The sexual abuse scandal, of course, has provided fuel for the fire of hatred that feeds some of these attacks. Whether because priests represent Christ, whom the world rejects, or because priests spiritually guide Catholics to oppose the world's immoral values and distorted truths or because the celibacy of Roman Catholic priests is a direct contradiction of the sexual license so prevalent in society today, the world seems intent on destroying the priesthood. Of course, we have Jesus' assurance that they will never succeed, since the very forces of hell shall not prevail against the Church (see Matthew 16:18). But try they do!

The media lead the attack. They have presented a grossly distorted picture of the sexual failings of priests. I once experienced the effects of this distortion. Dressed in my Franciscan habit, I was standing in a store when a stranger came up and asked me publicly, "Do you molest children?"

It goes without saying that any priest's betrayal of his people, the Church and the Lord through sexual abuse is a cause of great grief. Even one case of sexual abuse is intolerable. But many people in the media, enemies of the Church, know that the overwhelming majority of priests do not engage in any sexual abuse. They never report that it is only a small percentage of priests who are guilty of these crimes. Furthermore, they leave the impression that only Catholic priests commit these offenses and imply that priests do this because they are celibate.

We must respect our priests for their sacred vocation as "other Christs," if we cannot always respect them for who they are personally. The Church, in the persons of her bishops and priests, has faults and failings. Some have caused genuine scandal, and such scandal rightly must be condemned. Reparation legitimately must be made when harm has been done. But, on the other hand, there is a need for us to have an honest and balanced picture of the situation.

Respect the Priesthood

Saint Francis had great esteem, reverence and love for priests. He said that if he met a priest and an angel at the same moment, he would first greet the priest by kissing his hand, and then he would greet the angel. He never became a priest because he felt himself unworthy, although he did become a deacon.

Francis' great reverence for priests stemmed from his profound love and veneration for the Holy Eucharist, which he saw as intimately linked to the priesthood. He wrote about this in his *Testament*: "I refuse to consider their sins, because I can see the Son of God in them and they are better than I. I do this because in this world I cannot see the most high Son of God with my own eyes, except for his most holy Body and Blood which they receive and they alone administer to others."[11]

Pray for Priests

In response to the scandals and to the world's attacks, we must pray that our priests will always be Christlike, dedicated and preserved by God's grace in faithfulness to their call. Saint Thérèse of the Child Jesus entered Carmel, she said, to save souls and, above all, to pray for priests.

While we pray for our priests, they in turn must pray for the grace to stir up in their lives the gift of the Holy Spirit they received at their priestly ordination: "Hence I remind you to rekindle the gift of God that is within you through the laying on of my hands; for God did not give us a spirit of timidity but a spirit of power and love and self-control" (2 Timothy 1:6–7). The Holy Spirit will lead priests to great holiness in their vocation! 🕊

CHAPTER 8

Pastors and the Kingly Office of Jesus

THE KINGLY OR ROYAL OFFICE OF JESUS refers to His lordship or "governing" over the universe. Jesus has a threefold claim to be a king.

First, born a descendant of King David, He could claim the kingship of Israel. In fact, when Our Lady conceived Jesus in her womb at the Annunciation, the archangel Gabriel told her that "the Lord God will give to him the throne of his father David, and he will reign over the house of Jacob for ever" (Luke 1:32–33). Underscoring this, Scripture tells us that the inscription at the top of His cross read: "Jesus of Nazareth, the King of the Jews" (John 19:19).

Second, Jesus has the right to be king of all mankind because as God's only begotten Son become man, He holds the first place of honor and majesty over all creation. In His human nature He was the "first-born of all creation" (see Colossians 1:15). This fact moved Saint Paul to call Jesus the "last Adam" (see 1 Corinthians 15:45), the new Head of the human race.

Third, Jesus has the right to be king over all mankind because He is our Savior. He redeemed our fallen human race from the sentence of eternal damnation, the price of our sins. He gave us eternal life and therefore has the right to reign over us: Jesus "exercises his kingship by drawing all men to himself through his death and Resurrection" (*CCC*, #786).

TO RULE IS TO SERVE

Jesus, however, did not exercise His kingly office of governing in the manner of worldly leaders. In speaking with His apostles, He contrasted the world's approach to leadership with His own:

> You know that the rulers of the Gentiles lord it over them, and their great ones are tyrants over them. It will not be so among you; but whoever wishes to be great among you must be your servant, and whoever wishes to be first among you must be your slave; just as the Son of Man came not to be served but to serve, and to give his life as a ransom for many
>
> —MATTHEW 20:25–28, NRSV

Throughout His public ministry Jesus' governing style was apparent in His humble service to others. As He carried out His kingly mission, He fulfilled the prophet Isaiah's description of the Suffering Servant:[1] giving food to the hungry, drink to the thirsty, health to the sick, sight to the blind, comfort to the brokenhearted, liberty to captives, release to prisoners and the good news of salvation to the poor, while announcing a year of favor from the Lord (see Isaiah 53)!

Finally, as we have seen, when Jesus gave His apostles the power of the priesthood at the Last Supper, He showed them by an unmistakable example how they were to exercise that power: He washed their feet (see John 13:1–17). This Christian attitude is summed up in a traditional phrase: "To reign with Christ is to serve with Christ."

Christ established that the apostles together formed one apostolic college or body of leadership, with Peter at the head. In the same way He willed that the pope as Peter's successor and the bishops as the successors of the apostles would form one hierarchical or episcopal college, the body of bishops with the pope at the head. Together the pope and the bishops share Jesus' kingly office of governing or shepherding the Church. They form a hierarchy (literally, "government by holy ones") or sacred leadership, since Christ Himself established them to govern His Church. Their roles, however, are distinct.

THE POPE: SUPREME SHEPHERD OF THE FLOCK OF CHRIST

In a touching scene after the Resurrection, Jesus three times asked Peter to proclaim his love for Him in atonement for the three times Peter had denied Him on Holy Thursday (see John 21:15–17). Each time Peter renewed his love for Our Lord, Jesus gave him a new task: "feed my lambs," "tend my sheep," "feed my sheep." One who loves must always be ready to serve.

Jesus transformed Peter from a fisherman into a shepherd. The fisherman's only relationship to his fish is to catch them; that is basically where it ends. The shepherd, however, as we have seen, has a close and continuous relationship with his sheep. He leads them daily to food and water, he protects them from the ravages of wolves and thieves, and he seeks out the lost, carries the weak and binds up the injured. Jesus was now asking Peter to do all of these things: Peter had become the supreme shepherd of the flock of the Good Shepherd, the flock of Jesus Himself! As the *Catechism* makes clear: "The Lord made Simon alone, whom he names Peter, the 'rock' of his Church. He gave him the keys of his Church and instituted him shepherd of the whole flock" (#881).

THE PRIMACY OF THE POPE

The pope, divinely established as the vicar of Christ and the bishop of Rome (as the successor of Saint Peter), has by his very office the supreme authority to govern the Church. This authority extends not only to matters of faith and morals but also to matters affecting the discipline or daily routine of life in the Church. This authority is referred to as the "primacy of the pope," a dogma of the Roman Catholic Church defined by the First Vatican Council on July 18, 1870. This council solemnly defined the doctrine that by the will of Christ there has been a continuous line of successors to the office of Saint Peter and that the Roman pontiff does succeed in Peter's primacy over the universal Church.

> His authority as bishop is 'immediate,' that is to say, each member of the flock, of whatever rank, is required to accept the pastoral direction of the first shepherd. He is bishop of all the Church, of his fellow bishops and all the faithful, individually and collectively. The pope's authority and duty extend not only to the teaching of faith and moral doctrine, but also to whatever pertains

to the discipline and government of the Church throughout the world."[2]

This primacy of the pope is evident in Jesus entrusting two supreme powers to Peter: the "keys to the kingdom of heaven" as well as the power of "binding" and "loosing" on earth (see Matthew 16:19). These expressions signify, among other things, the authority to command others and to release them from obligations.[3]

This papal primacy is also seen in Jesus' words to Saint Peter to "strengthen your brethren" (the apostles) (see Luke 22:32). This is all the more significant since, except for the far more reprehensible betrayal by Judas, no other apostle formally denied knowing Our Lord, as Peter did in his threefold denial. We can see, therefore, that the primacy of the pope does not come from his personal holiness, nor would it be lost by lack of it. It comes immediately to him when, once being consecrated a bishop, he freely accepts the office of the papacy after being lawfully elected to it (see canon 332).

Papal primacy is not a matter of "honor," of recognizing the ancient dignity of the See of Rome established by Saint Peter so that the pope is merely an honorary "first among equals." Rather, the pope has real power over the universal Church as well as over particular churches (see canon 333, paragraph 1). He can freely exercise his "supreme, full, immediate and universal" authority (see canon 331) either in a personal way, on his own initiative, or in a collegial manner with all or some of the bishops (see canon 333, paragraph 2).

When the pope has acted by the primacy of his authority, there is neither recourse nor appeal against his judgment or decree (see canon 333, paragraph 3). After all, who would have the authority to reverse the pope's use of his primacy?

The Burden of Papal Primacy

This primacy of the pope makes him the perpetual and visible source and foundation of the Church's unity, both for the hierarchy (since he is head of the college of bishops) and for the laity (since he is the shepherd of the universal Church on earth). His task is by no means smooth sailing. (Even Peter had some very rough experiences on the Sea of Galilee with Jesus!) An old saying has it, it gets lonely at the top. No one is more at the top than the Holy Father carrying out the responsibilities of his office.

The remarks of two popes speak for themselves. Pope Paul VI was a close friend of Archbishop Fulton J. Sheen. In one of his recorded conferences, the archbishop referred to a conversation in which the pope told him: "I read my mail every night at midnight, just before I go to bed. In nine out of ten letters, there is always a thorn, so much so that when I rest my head on my pillow at night, I feel like I am placing it on a veritable crown of thorns!"

One can only imagine what these thorns were: probably accounts of persecution, imprisonment and torture, abandonment of the faith, scandal, lack of necessary vocations, conflicts and wars, famine and drought and every kind of human suffering! Pope Paul VI was the father in Christ of all these correspondents. He took their pain and suffering into his own heart.

A bishop told me of another incident. He was part of a group of American bishops who had come to visit Pope John

Paul II, as bishops do every five years. At one point the Holy Father was looking out the window in his quarters, overlooking St. Peter's Square. He turned unexpectedly to the bishop and said, "You have no idea how heavy the burden is that I carry."

These comments should remind us to pray daily for our Holy Father in gratitude for all he does (and suffers) for us and for the Church. We should pray for his personal welfare along with his special intentions. Finally, we should pray that the Holy Spirit will come to him, refresh him in body and spirit, give him the wisdom and courage necessary to persevere at the task, "whether convenient or inconvenient" (see 2 Timothy 4:2) and fill him with the joy and consolation that flow from hope in the resurrection of Jesus.

BISHOPS

The bishops, along with the pope, share the kingly office of Jesus in a unique way. They exercise their governing authority either communally in the college of bishops or individually, in the case of diocesan bishops, in their own dioceses. In both instances the bishops' authority must always be in agreement with the supreme authority of the pope.

THE COLLEGE OF BISHOPS

The pope, as we have seen, is the head of the college of bishops, just as Peter was head of the college of the apostles. The bishops are members of the episcopal college by virtue of their sacramental consecration. Through this consecration they share in the fullness of the priesthood of Christ, and they share in communion with the pope and one another in hierarchical leadership of the Church. In union with the pope and *never* without him, the college of bishops exercises supreme and full power over the universal Church (see canon 336).[4]

The collegial nature of the bishops' governing the Church with the pope was brought out at Vatican II, but it is evident throughout the whole history of the Church:

> Though Christ gave a true primacy to Peter, he was to shepherd the Church not in isolation, but in fraternal, collegial unity with his fellow apostles. In a similar way, the pope, as successor to St. Peter, governs the Church in collegial unity with his fellow bishops, successors of the apostolic college. Fully respecting the special role Christ wishes the Holy Father to undertake in His name, the bishops over the whole world cooperate with him in the care for all the Church.
>
> This "collegiality" has always been recognized in the living practice of the Church. Even in the earliest years of the Church, when dangers threatened the purity and unity of faith, the bishops gathered together in councils to make, with the assistance of the Holy Spirit (cf. Acts 15:28), decisions for the direction of the whole Church.
>
> Another expression of collegiality in antiquity was the great concern for "communion" among the various local churches and between each of them and the Roman See. They were linked together "in a bond of unity, charity and peace" (*Lumen gentium,* 22). The "communion" of bishops with one another was a sign and expression of the communion binding together the whole Church.[5]

There are two main expressions of the collegiality of the bishops. The first is in an ecumenical council, in which bishops from every part of the Church gather to discuss matters pertaining to Church doctrine or discipline. There have been twenty-one such councils held over the Church's history. Canon law states that it is the prerogative of the pope alone to summon, preside over (personally or through others), transfer, suspend or dissolve a council, determine its agenda— other bishops may add their own proposals with his approval—and approve its decrees (see canon 338).

A second expression of the bishops' acting in communion with the Holy Father and with each other is a synod of bishops. On September 15, 1965, during the final session of the Second Vatican Council, Pope Paul VI instituted the synod as a new form of collegial cooperation in the Church. A synod consists of a limited group of bishops who represent the whole college of bishops; they meet to discuss certain matters that the Holy Father proposes for discussion. They then offer him their advice and counsel.

In this way a synod of bishops assists the pope in the defense and development of faith and morals, in preserving and strengthening Church discipline and in considering questions concerning the mission of the Church in the world. A synod helps keep the Holy Father informed of the mind and concerns of bishops and faithful throughout the world.

Bishops in Their Own Dioceses

In the universal Catholic Church there are many local churches or dioceses. A diocesan bishop, known as the ordinary, governs the local church. Often the ordinary works with one or more auxiliary bishops or sometimes with a coadjutor bishop, who has the right to succeed the ordinary as the next bishop of the diocese. In reference to the governing role of the bishop, the Constitution on the Church says: "In the person of the bishops…the Lord Jesus Christ…is present in the midst of the faithful" (21). And, "The bishops, while loyally respecting the primacy and pre-eminence of their head [the pope], exercise their own proper authority for the good of their faithful, indeed even for the good of the whole Church, the organic structure and harmony of which are strengthened by the continual influence of the Holy Spirit" (22).

Diocesan bishops are true ambassadors and vicars of Christ. They should govern the particular or local church assigned to them by their counsels, exhortations and example, as well as by their hierarchical authority and sacred power. They exercise this power and authority personally in the name of Christ and always in agreement with the pope's supreme authority in the Church.

THE ROLE OF THE HOLY SPIRIT IN THE KINGLY MISSION OF PASTORS

In consecrated religious life—for example, that of priests and nuns, sisters and brothers—we often speak of those in authority as having "the grace of office." If the Lord gives a responsibility, in this case to shepherd His people by governing them, then He must provide the means to accomplish the task. He did this for His pastors when He sent the Holy Spirit to direct the work of His Church, to build it up until it reaches its fullness and perfection on His return at the end of the world.

THE POPE

In a special way the Holy Spirit gives the "grace of office" to those called to shepherd His flock, particularly the pope and bishops. The pope, since he has the primacy of authority in the Church, requires the special guidance of the Holy Spirit. He has been entrusted with the most important task on earth, to lead the Church in glorifying God and working for the eternal salvation of souls.

The pope has many responsibilities as he guides the Church in her daily life of prayer and discipline. One of the most important is the appointing of worthy bishops, faithful men who will be true spiritual shepherds of souls, for the different dioceses of the world. No man can be ordained a bishop nor be appointed the ordinary of a diocese without the express permission of the pope (see canon 377).

The pope must also encourage bishops, individually or as a region, when certain difficulties arise. Jesus told Peter, "Strengthen your brethren" (Luke 22:32), and, "Tend my sheep" (John 21:16). The pope must correct brother bishops when needed and even remove them from office if scandal or grave harm to souls threatens.

A pope's call for an ecumenical council of all the bishops is an extraordinary manifestation of his leadership role. Such a decision goes far beyond human judgment and insight, requiring the clear enlightenment of the Holy Spirit. When Pope John XXIII convoked the Second Vatican Council, he took the Church and the world by surprise. In a word that came to embody the thrust of the council, he called for *aggiornamento*—literally translated from Italian, as "updating"—so that the Church could deal effectively with contemporary society. The Church and the world were moving so far apart that the Church was in danger of losing the ability to dialogue effectively with the world.

Pope John Paul II said that Vatican Council II was the greatest spiritual event in the Catholic Church since Pentecost. Such a decision on the part of Pope John XXIII could not have been a result of human ingenuity or common sense. It was a decision that reflected the guidance and inspiration of the Holy Spirit.

The pope must also provide for the well-being of the entire people of God, not only through his teaching authority, as we shall see in the next chapter, but also through his governing authority. Pope John Paul II demonstrated this time and again. He restored, for example, a sense of respect and commitment to priestly life after a period in which priests and religious had given up their commitment in great numbers. He maintained the importance of priestly celibacy when it was under attack in many sectors of the Church. He has dealt with a variety of issues—involving life and death, the role of women today, the rights of the poor, Communism and the like—with a clarity of thought and determination of will that defy a purely human explanation.

Pope John Paul II was a pope truly open to the inspiration and guidance of the Holy Spirit. This is seen especially in his call to all the Church—hierarchy and laity, individuals and groups—to join in the task of a new evangelization, to proclaim Jesus anew to the world. One sensed a special light and direction of the Spirit of truth at work through this vicar of Christ.

The pope's concern reaches to people of various backgrounds, believers and nonbelievers alike. He requires the special guidance of the Holy Spirit to show himself a compassionate, understanding, yet uncompromising, father to all of God's people.

THE BISHOPS

Bishops, too, have "the grace of office," and what we have seen of the Holy Spirit's special guidance of the pope applies to them, with proper adjustment.

The Bishop's Role

Canon law mentions some of the more important obligations a diocesan bishop has in governing his diocese. These include being solicitous for all Christ's faithful entrusted to his care; showing an apostolic spirit and promoting the works of the apostolate; fostering a balanced ecumenism; showing a special concern for his priests and their needs; fostering vocations; praying for the people; defending the unity of the Catholic Church and upholding its discipline; making regular visitations of his diocese; and giving a good example to his priests and people (see canons 381–402). The *Catechism* states:

> The Good Shepherd ought to be the model and "form" of the bishops' pastoral office. Conscious of his own weaknesses, "the bishop…can have compassion for those who are ignorant and erring. He should not refuse to listen to his own subjects whose welfare he promotes as his very own children….The faithful…should be closely attached to the bishop as the Church is to Jesus Christ, and as Jesus Christ is to the Father."
>
> "Let all follow the bishop, as Jesus Christ follows

His Father, and the college of presbyters [priests] as the
apostles; respect the deacons as you do God's law. Let
no one do anything concerning the Church in separation
from the bishop." (*CCC*, #896)[6]

The bishop should fulfill his pastoral office of leadership out
of loving fidelity both to the Lord and to the Church as the
spouse of Christ. He should do so with vigilance, protecting
the flock committed to his care.

The principal celebrant at an episcopal ordination
invests the newly ordained bishop with two significant
insignia of his new office. The celebrant places the episcopal
ring on the ring finger of the new bishop and says: "Take this
ring, the seal of your fidelity. With faith and love protect the
bride of God, his holy Church."[7] This is the bishop's call to
loving fidelity, sharing Jesus' own spousal relationship to the
Church. As Jesus the divine bridegroom loved the Church,
His spouse, and laid down His life for her, so now must the
new bishop.

The newly ordained bishop also receives a pastoral staff
or crosier. As the celebrant gives him his pastoral staff, he
says: "Take this staff as a sign of your pastoral office: keep
watch over the whole flock in which the Holy Spirit has
appointed you to shepherd the Church of God."[8] This
reminds the new bishop of his role as the spiritual shepherd
of his flock in imitation of Saint Peter and his successors.

We must pray for our bishops as they go about their difficult work, which is so important to the welfare of the
Church. As an old saying puts it: "The miter weighs heavy on
the head of him who wears it!" We should pray daily that our
bishops have a generous love that will enable them to forget

themselves, to give of themselves in constant service as they meet the needs of all in their flock. This spirit of sacrifice will be tested as they encounter the misunderstandings, conflicts and even opposition that will inevitably come their way. The life of a bishop is truly a share in the cross of Christ.

The Bishops' Receipt of a Generous Outpouring of the Holy Spirit

The apostles themselves needed to receive "power from on high" (Luke 24:49) before they could go forth and witness to Jesus "to the ends of the earth" (Acts 1:8). The bishops, as successors of the apostles, need this same power of the Holy Spirit to stir their love and courage.

At an episcopal ordination the new bishop receives the Spirit in generous measure when, after the prayer of consecration, the principal ordaining bishop anoints the head of the newly ordained bishop with sacred chrism. This anointing with the Church's most holy oil is an external symbol of the internal outpouring of the Holy Spirit, which the bishop has just received through his episcopal consecration. As he pours the oil on the head of the new bishop, the principal ordaining bishop invokes a blessing from the Lord: "God has brought you to share the high priesthood of Christ. May he pour out on you the oil of mystical anointing and enrich you with spiritual blessing."[9]

The bishops should invoke the Holy Spirit's help constantly so that they do not end up relying on human resources alone, which prove inadequate when put to the test. A bishop who relies on human wisdom alone when the wisdom of the Spirit is needed may incur the reproach of the Lord to Peter:

"You are not on the side of God, but of men" (Matthew 16:23). If he fails to have the courage to guide his flock, he may hear the Lord say, "O man of little faith, why did you doubt?" (Matthew 14:31).

A bishop can draw strength and consolation from reflecting prayerfully and trustingly on the words from the prayer of his episcopal consecration, a prayer directed to God the Father:

> So now pour out upon the chosen one
> that power which is from you,
> the governing Spirit
> whom you gave to your beloved Son, Jesus Christ,
> the Spirit given by him to the holy apostles,
> who founded the Church in every place to be your
>   temple
> for the unceasing glory and praise of your name.
> Father, you know all hearts.
> You have chosen your servant for the office of bishop.
> May he be shepherd to your holy flock,
> and high priest blameless in your sight,
> ministering to you night and day;
> may he always gain the blessing of your favor
> and offer the gifts of your holy Church.
> Through the Spirit who gives the grace of high
>   priesthood,
> grant him the power
> to forgive sins as you have commanded,
> to assign ministries as you have decreed,
> and to loose every bond by the authority which you
>   gave to your apostles.
> May he be pleasing to you by his gentleness and purity
>   of heart,
> presenting a fragrant offering to you,

through Jesus Christ, your Son,
through whom glory and power and honor are yours
with the Holy Spirit
in your holy Church,
now and forever. Amen.[10]

CHAPTER 9

Pastors and the Prophetic Office of Jesus

THE PROPHETIC OFFICE OF JESUS refers to His teaching authority and mission. Jesus, the eternal Word who became flesh (see John 1:14), came from the Father to be His final Word of revelation to us:

> In many and various ways God spoke of old to our fathers by the prophets; but in these last days he has spoken to us by a Son, whom he appointed the heir of all things, through whom also he created the world. He reflects the glory of God and bears the very stamp of his nature, upholding the universe by his word of power.
>
> —HEBREWS 1:1–3

Jesus came as the fulfillment of all the old covenant hopes and promises. By His saving death and resurrection and by His sending of the Holy Spirit from the Father, Jesus initiated the new covenant, which will never end. He not only proclaimed the truth by all He did and taught, but He Himself was and ever remains the very fullness of truth.

Furthermore, He tells us that this is the truth that sets us free (see John 8:32). It is a freedom, first of all, from ignorance, error and falsehood. It is also a freedom to become the children of God we are called to be.

THE HIERARCHY AND THE PROPHETIC OFFICE OF THE CHURCH

The hierarchy—the pope and the bishops in union with him—are the primary teachers in the Roman Catholic Church. As the successors of Saint Peter and the apostles, they officially exercise the prophetic office of preaching and teaching within the Church and for the Church as a whole.

THE PROPHETIC OFFICE: THE PRIMARY RESPONSIBILITY OF PASTORS

Our risen Lord clearly conferred upon His apostles the mission of preaching and teaching.

> And he [Jesus] said to them: "Go into all the world and preach the gospel to the whole creation."
>
> —MARK 16:15

> And Jesus came and said to them, "All authority in heaven and on earth has been given to me. Go therefore and make disciples of all nations, baptizing them in the name of the Father and of the Son and of the Holy Spirit, teaching them to observe all that I have commanded you; and lo, I am with you always, to the close of the age."
>
> —MATTHEW 28:18–20

In fulfillment of Jesus' command, Peter and the apostles "went forth and preached everywhere" (Mark 16:20). They lost no time in fulfilling their prophetic office, beginning with preaching on Pentecost: "But Peter, standing with the eleven, lifted up his voice and addressed them, 'Men of Judea and all who dwell in Jerusalem, let this be known to you, and give ear to my words'" (Acts 2:14).

The Holy Spirit, the Spirit of truth, had just come down upon the apostles, filling them with His gifts of wisdom, understanding, knowledge and courage. "Tongues as of fire" accompanied His coming and rested on the heads of those present in the Upper Room (see Acts 2:3). These "tongues as of fire" represented the power of the Spirit of truth Himself, who would vivify and intensify their preaching and teaching.

In addition, the Spirit of truth recalled for them what Jesus had taught them (see John 14:26). He also set them free from the fear that led them to lock the doors of the Upper Room, even after they had seen the Lord Jesus risen from the dead (see John 20:19–26). So we read that the Holy Spirit prompted all the disciples to speak boldly about the Lord Jesus and His message of salvation (see Acts 2:4, 11).

Saint Paul's Concern for the Office of Teaching

The apostles wanted the prophetic office in the Church to be carried out faithfully and effectively, in order to spread the truth about Jesus, the Incarnate Son of God and Savior of the world. This is evident in the writings of Saint Paul, especially in his Letters to Timothy and Titus. These two early disciples were close companions of Paul in his missionary work and became elders (or bishops) in the early Church. They received the Holy Spirit at their episcopal consecration by the laying on of hands, a prayerful gesture by the ordaining bishop that calls down the Holy Spirit upon the men being consecrated.

Saint Paul wrote to his two young companions, instructing and encouraging them in their teaching office. He told Timothy that a bishop should be "an apt teacher" (1 Timothy 3:2) and reminded the young man not to be intimidated by those who would criticize or contradict him because of his youth:

> If you put these instructions before the brethren, you will be a good minister of Christ Jesus, nourished on the words of the faith and of the good doctrine which you have followed. Have nothing to do with godless and silly myths. Train yourself in godliness.... Command and teach these things. Let no one despise your youth, but set the believers an example in speech and conduct, in love, in faith, in purity. Till I come, attend to the public reading of scripture, to preaching, to teaching. Do not neglect the gift you have, which was given you by prophetic utterance when the elders laid their hands upon you.... Take heed to yourself and to your teaching: hold to that, for by so doing you will save both yourself and your hearers.
>
> —1 TIMOTHY 4:6–7, 11–14, 16

Saint Paul also urged Timothy to "stir into flame" (2 Timothy 1:6, NEB) by prayer and zeal the Spirit of truth within him, for God does not give a cowardly spirit but "a spirit of power and love and self-control" (see 2 Timothy 1:7). The great apostle then prepared his young disciple for the suffering he would inevitably endure from "wicked people and imposters" who "go from bad to worse, deceiving others and being deceived" (see 2 Timothy 3:13, NRSV). He exhorted Timothy to be faithful to his apostolic charge:

> I charge you.... preach the word, be urgent in season and out of season, convince, rebuke, and exhort, be unfailing in patience and in teaching. For the time is coming when people will not endure sound teaching, but having itching ears they will accumulate for themselves teachers to suit their own likings, and will turn away from listening to the truth and wander into myths. As for you, always be steady, endure suffering, do the work of an evangelist, fulfil your ministry.
>
> —2 TIMOTHY 4:2–5

Finally the apostle to the Gentiles pointed to his own good example and dedication as a model for the young bishop:

> For this gospel I was appointed a preacher and apostle and teacher, and therefore I suffer as I do. But I am not ashamed, for I know whom I have believed, and I am sure that he is able to guard until that Day what has been entrusted to me. Follow the pattern of the sound words which you have heard from me, in the faith and love which are in Christ Jesus; guard the truth which has been entrusted to you by the Holy Spirit who dwells within us.
>
> —2 TIMOTHY 1:11–14

The teaching office that Jesus gave to Peter and the apostles has been passed on over the centuries to their successors, the popes and bishops. Vatican Council II, as we will see, clearly restated this essential dogma of the Catholic Church.

THE POPE: SUPREME, INFALLIBLE TEACHER

Jesus made Peter alone the foundation of His Church and gave to him alone the keys of the kingdom of heaven (see Matthew 16:18–19). Furthermore, He appointed him to be shepherd over the whole of His flock (see John 21:15–17). These actions clearly indicate Saint Peter's primacy and authority over the whole Church.

In exercising his supreme teaching office, the pope enjoys a special prerogative called infallibility.[1] This means that the pope, through the Holy Spirit, is kept free from error when declaring certain doctrine to be dogma of the Catholic Church. The Catholic people are bound, in conscience, to believe this dogma by the assent of faith.

Infallibility assures that what the pope is saying is truly the teaching of Jesus Christ. When the pope teaches in this manner he is teaching *ex cathedra*, a Latin phrase meaning "from the chair" of Saint Peter. The Second Vatican Council stated its teaching on this point very clearly:

> The Roman Pontiff, head of the college of bishops, enjoys this infallibility in virtue of his office, when, as supreme pastor and teacher of all the faithful—who confirms his brethren in the faith—he proclaims in an absolute decision a doctrine pertaining to faith or morals. For that reason his definitions are rightly said to be irreformable by their very nature and not by reason of the assent of the Church, in as much as they were made with the assistance of the Holy Spirit promised to him in the person of blessed Peter himself; and as a consequence they are in no way in need of the approval of others, and do not admit of appeal to any other tribunal. For in such a case the Roman Pontiff does not utter a

> pronouncement as a private person, but rather does he
> expound and defend the teaching of the Catholic faith as
> the supreme teacher of the universal Church, in whom
> the Church's charism of infallibility is present in a singu-
> lar way. (*Lumen gentium,* 25)

The prerogative of infallibility assures that the Church will
never lose, distort, misunderstand or misrepresent any
authentic teaching or doctrine that Christ has revealed and
that constitutes part of the deposit of faith. This guarantees
that the Church will preserve intact the deposit of faith, safeguarding it from any addition, subtraction or error.

When the pope teaches with the authority of his
supreme magisterium or teaching office, and he proposes a
doctrine "in conformity with revelation itself" and as the
teaching of Christ, "all are bound to adhere" and "are obliged
to submit" to his definitions (see *Lumen gentium,* 25). The
pope's teachings do not get their binding force from a majority vote of Catholics or bishops or any other group in the
Church. They demand assent because the Spirit of truth
assures that they are true and contain no error.

Consequences of Papal Infallibility

This prerogative of infallibility has saved the Catholic Church
from two tragic difficulties.

*Infallibility preserves the Church from relativism and contradictory
teaching.* The Church has avoided (at least in her official teaching) a relativistic approach to truth. Such an approach holds
that any interpretation of a teaching is acceptable as long as
one is comfortable with it. It doesn't matter if it contradicts

someone else's interpretation, because that person's interpretation is equally acceptable!

The Church in her official teaching has been spared the multiplicity of contradictory beliefs that inevitably follow when people either are left to personal interpretation of Scripture and doctrine or must rely on consensus to establish their beliefs. Archbishop Fulton Sheen often said that even if nobody believes it, the truth is the truth, and even if everybody believes it, error is error!

Infallibility preserves the Church from skepticism. Papal infallibility also protects the Catholic Church from the skepticism that occurs when, faced with many conflicting opinions, people are unsure of exactly what Jesus has revealed. Both relativism and skepticism would pose insurmountable problems, especially since Jesus tells us we must live by what He teaches if we are to enter into eternal life. How can we live by what He teaches unless we are first sure what He taught? Papal infallibility, guaranteed by the Spirit of Truth, gives us this necessary assurance.

The Burden of Papal Infallibility

It takes great courage for the pope to proclaim time and again the truths of Christ in the face of a world—and even many in the Church—that does not want to hear his message. When Pope John Paul II was in South America, a reporter remarked to him that he, the pope, often said things that upset people, things they didn't want to hear. The Holy Father agreed, noting that people still needed to hear those things and that was precisely why he said them.

THE TEACHING ROLE AND RESPONSIBILITY
OF THE BISHOPS

The bishops of the Church are also shepherds in their own dioceses. They enjoy the special guidance of the Spirit of truth by their very office. When the bishops teach in union with the pope, they share in the prerogative of infallibility.

The responsibility to teach true Catholic doctrine to the flock is emphasized during the impressive ceremony of a bishop's ordination. Just before the prayer of consecration, the principal consecrating bishop places an open book of the Gospels over the head of the bishop-elect. This signifies that as a bishop—a successor of the apostles—he is to continue the apostolic preaching of Jesus.

After his ordination the new bishop receives various insignia that symbolize his new office. One of the most important is the book of the Gospels. The principal ordaining bishop addresses him with the words: "Receive the Gospel and go preach to the people committed to you, for God is powerful to increase his grace in you."[2]

Saint Paul and the Teaching Role of Bishops

Paul's Letter to Titus and First and Second Letters to Timothy are traditionally called his pastoral epistles. We have seen that in his First Letter to Timothy, Saint Paul states that a man who would be a bishop should be "an apt teacher" (1 Timothy 3:2). He further urges his young disciple Timothy to be serious about his pastoral duties of governing the church community at Ephesus (see 1 Timothy 1:3) and about his responsibility to teach carefully and constantly (see 1 Timothy 4:11–16).

Bishops are the primary teachers of the Word of God to the faithful placed in their pastoral care but priests, theologians and religious educators within their dioceses assist them. Furthermore, the bishop is responsible for correcting wrong teaching, a point made clear when he receives his episcopal ring at his ordination: "Take this ring," the presiding bishop tells him, "the seal of your fidelity. With faith and love protect the bride of God, His holy Church."[3] The bishop must stand as a faithful teacher, turning his flock away from false teaching and toward the truth.

People's unwillingness to hear the truth is no less an issue today than it was in Paul's time, when he told Timothy that the time was fast approaching when people would want to hear only teachings that would let them live as they pleased (see 2 Timothy 4:2–5). As Archbishop Fulton Sheen used to say, people don't become heretics for the way they want to think but for the way they want to live!

The restless age that Paul described certainly matches our own. The firm guidance and clear teaching of good bishops will hold the Church on the right course. Paul advises them to heed three points.

First, the bishop must continue to preach patiently even when there is resistance to the message. The truth must be proclaimed. God will see to its bearing fruit, and that requires patience on the preacher's part.

Second, the bishop must correct (errors and ignorance), reprove (falsehood) and appeal (to truth, faith, sincerity and even common sense). He should use different approaches in different circumstances. The bishop, like a good physician, must apply the medicine that works best in the situation.

Third, he must neither be intimidated by the fear of bad press nor remain silent when the truth of the Catholic Church is misrepresented through ignorance and even deliberately attacked or distorted publicly. He may be criticized as "unfair" for not engaging in "dialogue" about the issue in question, for not giving "due process" or ultimately for not agreeing with or at least tolerating the opposite opinion. Some people can become so sensitive that they interpret any resistance to their ideas or any "no" in the most pejorative terms. The bishop must be a man of courage and principle. He must stay with his tasks of preaching and teaching whether convenient or inconvenient. The Spirit of truth will be his support.

Called to Suffer in Witness to the Truth

Saint Paul also told Timothy that whoever wants to be a bishop aspires to "a noble task" (1 Timothy 3:1). Archbishop Sheen commented that Paul could make such a statement because a bishop in the early Church almost inevitably would die a martyr's death!

The archbishop added that today the martyrdom of bishops comes in different ways. Perhaps the most painful is the opposition to Christ's message that bishops encounter as they faithfully proclaim the Good News. Jesus warned about such "trials" before rulers, who in present times could be presidents, governors, politicians—Catholic and non-Catholic alike. The promise of Jesus is the bishops' consolation if they proclaim His truths and those of His Church in love, for He said: "What you are to say will be given to you in that hour; for it is not you who speak, but the Spirit of your Father speaking through you" (Matthew 10:19–20).

Saint Augustine adds a further consolation. He wrote that whenever he teaches as a bishop faithful to Christ's doctrine, he teaches with Christ's authority. "The Lord will help me to speak the truth if I do not speak on my own authority. For if I speak on my own authority, I will be a shepherd nourishing myself and not the sheep. However, if my words are the Lord's, then he is nourishing you no matter who speaks."[4]

CHAPTER **10**

The Laity Share the Threefold Mission of Jesus

SINCE ALL THE FAITHFUL are "baptized into Christ Jesus" (Romans 6:3), they share in His priestly, kingly and prophetic offices: "The Christian faithful...since they have become sharers in Christ's priestly, prophetic, and royal office in their own manner,...are called to exercise the mission which God has entrusted to the Church to fulfill in the world, in accord with the condition proper to each one" (canon 204).[1]

How do the laity share the threefold office of Jesus Christ?

THE LAITY SHARE JESUS' PRIESTLY OFFICE

The Holy Spirit helps each baptized Christian to carry out his or her priestly office. This is seen first in regard to prayer. The priestly prayer of the faithful springs from and rests on faith. Faith is ultimately a belief in God; although we do not see God, we know, love and pray to Him. It is the Holy Spirit who produces this faith in us! Saint Paul assures us, "No one can say 'Jesus is Lord' except by the Holy Spirit" (1 Corinthians 12:3).

This same Holy Spirit, the "Teacher within," as Pope John Paul II called Him, fills us with the assurance of our status as children of God: The Spirit Himself bears "witness with our spirit that we are children of God" (Romans 8:16). From this conviction of our filial relationship springs our claim to call God *Father* because, as Saint Paul says, we "did not receive the spirit of slavery to fall back into fear, but...the spirit of sonship" through which we cry out, "Abba, Father" (Romans 8:15).

It is the Holy Spirit's role to form all the faithful into a priestly people and lead them, both as individuals and as a community, in the work of salvation and sanctification. In this way the Church truly becomes God's instrument in the work of saving and sanctifying all peoples, for Christ died on the cross for all and calls all to eternal life. The laity become "a spiritual house and a holy priesthood" (*CCC*, #784). Joined to Jesus in the work of sanctification—of themselves and of the world—they worship God, especially through participation in the eucharistic celebration and adoration. Furthermore, the laity also offer "spiritual sacrifices" (1 Peter 2:5) in daily life.

> Hence the laity, dedicated as they are to Christ and anointed by the Holy Spirit, are marvelously called and prepared so that even richer fruits of the Spirit may be produced in them. For all their works, prayers and apostolic undertakings, family and married life, daily work, relaxation of mind and body, if they are accomplished in the Spirit—indeed even the hardships of life if patiently borne—all these become spiritual sacrifices acceptable to God through Jesus Christ. In the celebration of the Eucharist these may most fittingly be offered to the Father along with the body of the Lord. And so, wor-

shipping everywhere by their holy actions, the laity consecrate the world itself to God. (*Lumen gentium,* 34)

How do the laity achieve this? What gives their spiritual sacrifices transforming power?

The answer lies in the fact that these sacrifices are
accomplished in the Spirit. Paul reminds us that it is God who
brings about in our lives both the desire to do good deeds and
then the actual doing of these good deeds (see Philippians
2:13). It is the Holy Spirit, then, who first moves us to offer
our spiritual sacrifices by inspiring us to do them. He next
moves our will by His grace to carry out the good deeds He
inspired us to do. He further motivates us to offer these spiritual sacrifices for the greater glory of God and for our salvation and sanctification, as well as for that of our brothers and
sisters in Christ. As our holiness increases, the Holy Spirit
attunes our minds to listen more carefully to His inspirations,
and He inflames our wills with the fire of His love to carry out
those inspirations more consistently and ardently.

THE LAITY SHARE JESUS' KINGLY OFFICE

We have seen how Jesus exercised His kingly or royal office in
the form of service. The laity share in Jesus' kingly office
when they imitate Him and serve others as He did. In fact,
they are mysteriously serving Christ Himself, for He tells us
in the Gospel, "Truly, I say to you, as you did it to one of the
least of these my brethren, you did it to me" (Matthew 25:40).

Mother Teresa of Calcutta would often say that Jesus
comes in distressing disguise: as the poor, hungry, thirsty,
naked, homeless, sick or imprisoned. Whenever we assist
those in need, we assist Jesus Himself. She also made the

point that humanity can't really do anything for God in heaven because in heaven He has all that He needs. So He became man, making it possible for us to help Him. He said, "I was hungry,...thirsty,...naked,...ill."

Vatican Council II teaches clearly: "The Church encompasses with her love all those who are afflicted by human misery and she recognizes in those who are poor and who suffer, the image of her poor and suffering founder. She does all in her power to relieve their need and in them she strives to serve Christ" (*Lumen gentium*, 8).

The Holy Spirit moves the laity to share Jesus' mission of service. It is by the light of faith that we recognize Jesus when He comes "in distressing disguise," and it is by love that we are moved to serve His needs. Someone without faith and the love that must go with it would easily miss the Lord hidden behind the person in need.

One day in India a journalist watching Mother Teresa care for a man with gangrene told her that he wouldn't do that for a million dollars. "Even I wouldn't do it for that amount," Mother Teresa answered. "However, I do it out of love for God. This poor suffering man represents the body of Christ for me." Mother Teresa had the light of love from the Holy Spirit and so was able to see what the journalist missed.[2]

THE LAITY SHARE JESUS' PROPHETIC OFFICE

Through baptism and confirmation the laity share in the teaching role of Jesus and the Church. By word and example, person-to-person or through the media, the laity bring Jesus' message of salvation as well as the teachings of the Catholic

Church into the domain that is specifically theirs (as distinct from the domain of the clergy).

This domain encompasses the home and family circle, the marketplace with its technological advances and challenges, the civil structures and political arena of society and the cultural, educational and recreational areas of human life. In all these the laity are "the salt of the earth" (Matthew 5:13) and "the light of the world" (Matthew 5:14), reflecting the light—Jesus Himself—into human society in all its dimensions.

The Second Vatican Council stated: "Christ is the great prophet who proclaimed the kingdom of the Father both by the testimony of his life and by the power of his word. Until the full manifestation of his glory, he fulfills this prophetic office, not only by the hierarchy who teach in his name and by his power, but also by the laity. He accordingly both establishes them as witnesses and provides them with the sense of the faith (*sensus fidei*) and the grace of the word" (*Lumen gentium*, 35). The council here stresses three points regarding the laity's proclaiming the mystery of Christ that is the gospel message.

The Power of Witness

First it mentions the power of witness or good example, the most potent form of evangelization. Christians who practice what they preach give silent testimony to the truth. This testimony affects observers differently: it strengthens those who already believe; it enlightens those who are searching for the truth; it prods those who have neglected their faith; it challenges those who reject God and His truth. It would be hard to estimate, for example, the full effect of Mother Teresa's work. Her life of love, compassion, faith and dedication had worldwide appeal.

The witness of Catholic laity is all-embracing and transforms even the most ordinary circumstances of life: the family, the school, the office, travel, recreation and so on. Inspired and strengthened by the Holy Spirit, laypeople bring the values and virtues of Christian life—truth, honesty, chastity, charity, compassion, justice, kindness and more—into the center of human experience. Wherever they are, the laity consecrate and transform the world by the holiness of their lives. They proclaim in deed and word what Pope John Paul II called "the culture of life" to offset the dehumanizing and degrading "culture of death" that prevails in modern secular society.

The Sense of Faith

Second, Vatican II points out that Jesus has given His Church the *sensus fidei* or "sense of faith," a grace shared by the hierarchy and the laity. The sense of faith is a sensitivity to truth and anti-truth given by the Holy Spirit in matters of faith and morals. By it we can recognize truth while at the same time discerning error in its many forms.

This sense of faith helps to ensure the infallibility of the Church: the whole body of the faithful, hierarchy and laity, cannot all be in error at the same time.

> The whole body of the faithful who have an anointing that comes from the holy one (cf. 1 John 2:20, 27) cannot err in matters of belief. This characteristic is shown in the supernatural appreciation of the faith (*sensus fidei*) of

the whole people, when, "from the bishops to the last of the faithful" they manifest a universal consent in matters of faith and morals. (*Lumen gentium*, 12).

The Grace of the Word

Third, Vatican II teaches that the laity have "the grace of the word" to help them fulfill their role in the prophetic office of Jesus. This grace of the word applies primarily to Sacred Scripture's power to transform those who carry it within them. The Word of God in the Bible is "inspired," which means it is "breathed into" by the breath of the Holy Spirit. When we read the Word of God with faith, devotion and proper understanding, it becomes a living Word in us, the vivifying breath of God in us.

Saint Paul reminds us to "let the word of Christ dwell in you richly" (Colossians 3:16), where it will transform our values and attitudes. We begin to have the mind of Christ (see Philippians 2:5) and the heart of Christ formed in us by the Holy Spirit.

The Word of God then becomes a means of evangelizing others. If they are open to hear God's word—open in mind and heart, and not closed by prejudice or pride—the Scriptural word brings them to Jesus and to the Catholic Church. Saint Paul wrote to his young disciple Timothy about the importance of Scripture in the prophetic ministry:

> But…from childhood you have been acquainted with the sacred writings which are able to instruct you for salvation through faith in Christ Jesus. All scripture is inspired by God and profitable for teaching, for reproof, for correction, and for training in righteousness, that

the man of God may be complete, equipped for every
good work.

—2 TIMOTHY 3:15–17

What is said of the inspired Word of God in Sacred Scripture
extends to the authentic teachings of the Church. Such teachings are, in a broad sense, part of the grace of the word. When
we observe Church teaching in faith and morals, it guides our
growth in relation to God and in living a virtuous Christian
life. We can then share these teachings either formally—as a
teacher would in a classroom setting, for example—or infor-
mally, such as when we speak of Christ to people in a discussion group or in spontaneous conversation. In the following
chapters we will look at various forms of teaching within the
Church community.

PART V

The Spirit of Truth and Those in
Various Teaching Ministries

CHAPTER 11

Special Teachers in Church History

THROUGHOUT THE HISTORY OF THE CHURCH, the Spirit of truth has raised up many special teachers to carry out Christ's mission to teach "all nations" (see Matthew 28:18–20). In every age the Holy Spirit has distributed His gifts as He wills (see 1 Corinthians 12:11), inspiring outstanding individuals as well as groups and movements to meet the challenges of the Church in proclaiming and defending the truth of her teachings. Let's look briefly at some of these individuals and movements.

THE FATHERS OF THE CHURCH

We begin with the Fathers of the Church, the first outstanding teachers in Catholic Church history and the most important: they bear witness to the Church's earliest understanding of the deposit of faith as given by Christ and the apostles. The fathers are our vital link with the apostles themselves. They are the first Christian teachers to know and interpret Scripture and other apostolic teachings. Their witness, therefore, plays a foundational role regarding the authentic sacred tradition of the Catholic Church.

Who are the fathers of the Church, and where did the title come from? In biblical and early Christian usage, the title *father* was applied to teachers of the faith because they were considered fathers to their students. For example, Saint Paul says of himself: "For though you have countless guides in Christ, you do not have many fathers. For I became your father in Christ Jesus through the gospel" (1 Corinthians 4:15).

In the second century Saint Irenaeus of Lyons (d.c. 202), one of the earliest Church fathers, wrote in a similar way: "For when any person has been taught from the mouth of another, he is termed the son of him who instructs him, and the latter [is called] his father."[1]

Eventually the bishop was called father since, by virtue of his office, he was the teacher of the faithful. Later, during the doctrinal disputes of the fourth century, the title was extended to other Church writers who were accepted as representatives of the tradition of the Church. For example, Saint Augustine cited Saint Jerome as a father or witness to the traditional doctrine of original sin, although he was not a bishop.

The Contribution of Saint Vincent of Lerins

Saint Vincent of Lerins (d.c. 445), himself a father of the Church, described who was a father and who was not: "Fathers [were]...those...who, each in his own time and place, remaining in the unity of communion and of the faith, were accepted as approved masters."[2]

Saint Vincent helped set the stage for naming the four essential elements necessary for one to be declared a father of the Church: orthodoxy in doctrine—a father had to teach what the Catholic Church taught; holiness of life—a father had to be known for his sanctity; antiquity—a father had to have lived in approximately the first seven hundred years of Christianity; and ecclesiastical approval—the Church in some way had to recognize the person's contribution. If any of these elements were missing, a person would be simply an ecclesiastical writer.

Saint Vincent of Lerins also stated the importance of the fathers of the Church as witnesses of authentic Church teaching and tradition. He formulated a principle known as the "proof from the fathers": "Whatever has been sown by the fidelity of the Fathers in this husbandry of God's Church, the same ought to be cultivated and taken care of by the industry of their children, the same ought to flourish and ripen, the same ought to advance and go forward to perfection."[3]

This proof from the fathers is obviously very important for determining authentic Church teaching. The fathers themselves, whenever they wrote or taught doctrine, did not just assert a doctrine but carefully showed how it was connected to the apostles. As if following an unbroken chain backward link by link, they would appeal over a span of centuries from father back to another father back to still another father, until they reached back to the apostles and Our Lord Himself. This was "proof" that the doctrine they were teaching came unchanged from Jesus through the apostles.

Some Particulars About the Fathers

The Spirit of truth raised up veritable giants of the faith in the fathers of the Church. It would be impossible to summarize their contributions, but a few are worth mentioning.

Some of the fathers, known as apologists, defended the Church against false accusations, particularly during the time of the Roman persecutions. They almost always died as martyrs, giving the ultimate witness to Christ.

Others were associated with the first Christian schools of theology. Origen (d. 254), for example, was a great Scripture scholar and the author of *On First Principles*, probably the first Christian manual of theology. He at one time headed the first Christian school, located at Alexandria, Egypt. He insisted that a person could study and interpret Sacred Scripture correctly only if he spent time in prayer; adhered to the *regula fidei* or "rule of faith" (in other words, followed Church Tradition) and used other helps, such as the study of languages, for guidance.

Still other fathers defended the Catholic Church's teaching against heresy. In the process they often influenced the formulation of true Catholic doctrine at various regional gatherings of bishops and especially at ecumenical councils, the full gatherings of bishops. Saint Athanasius, bishop of Alexandria (d. 373), was the great opponent of Arianism, the heresy that denied the divinity of Christ. He played a major role at the ecumenical Council of Nicea in A.D. 325, helping to formulate the expression of Catholic doctrine that we profess to this day in the Nicene Creed at Mass.

Saint Augustine, for his part, wrote prolifically on Catholic doctrine, producing such masterpieces as his fifteen-volume *On the Trinity*. He did so while opposing heresies, like Pelagianism and Donatism, and shepherding his flock faithfully as bishop of Hippo in North Africa. Augustine also wrote one of the first catechisms.

THE SCHOLASTICS

After the era of the fathers of the Church, the Holy Spirit raised up teachers referred to as the scholastics or schoolmen. The golden age of scholasticism occurred during the High and Late Middle Ages (around A.D. 1050 to 1450), in times and circumstances very different from those in which the fathers lived. There were no major heresies or persecutions of the Church. The turmoil of the barbarian invasions had ended, while the threat from the Muslims had quieted down. Europe was basically Christian and at peace. In this climate learning flourished.

The Catholic Church played an important role in this revival of learning. Even prior to the rise of scholasticism, the Church had preserved much of the wisdom of ancient times. For example, during the Early Middle Ages—also called the Dark or Heroic Middle Ages, around A.D. 500 to 1050—monks painstakingly copied books by hand in their scriptoria, or copy rooms, preserving many ancient works from extinction.

This new era began with Saint Anselm of Canterbury (d. 1109), the father of scholasticism. It was he who opened the way for theological reflection on traditional Church teachings by stressing the use of reason in the sphere of faith. Like Saint Augustine, he was inspired by the principle that faith seeks understanding. This principle means that while we hold firmly to divinely revealed truth by a lively and unconditional faith, we can also penetrate its content further by exercising all the resources and power of natural intelligence.

Factors Contributing to Scholasticism

Intellectual and spiritual ferment, especially in the late twelfth and early thirteenth centuries, contributed to the rise of scholasticism. Some other major factors were:

The philosophy of Aristotle. The early fathers and other Church teachers used the philosophy of Plato to help express Christian teachings. Plato's philosophy was mystical; you can think of it as a way of the heart, with its intuitive vision and grasp of reality. The rediscovery of Aristotle through the Arabic philosophers Avicenna and Averroes opened new avenues of thought.

Aristotle's philosophy, by contrast, was the way of the mind, stressing a logical or dialectical approach to grasping and expressing reality. Gradually Aristotelian logic and reasoning surpassed Plato's intuitive mysticism as the predominant philosophy, especially because Saint Thomas Aquinas (d. 1274), the greatest of the scholastics, used it extensively.

The summas. The scholastics also tended to produce summas—essentially, reference books used as handbooks in schools—which disseminated their thinking. These large volumes of theology were called *summae sententiarum*, meaning "summaries of [theological] statements." In them the scholastics attempted to present the teachings of the Church fathers in a systematic, logical manner. For example, Peter Lombard (d. 1160) wrote *The Four Books of Sentences*, which served for about two centuries as the basic theological textbook of schools. The most famous and influential work, however, was the *Summa Theologica* of Saint Thomas Aquinas.

The rise of universities. The growth of universities, most established by the Catholic Church, also fueled the scholastic movement. These places of learning, found in such cities as Paris, Oxford and Cologne, became centers of theological speculation, discussion, debate and teaching. The schools, with their outstanding philosophy and theology teachers, enabled the Church to deepen her understanding and expression of what Christ had revealed and the Catholic Church had traditionally taught.

The rise of the mendicant orders. The rise of mendicant or begging orders, such as the Dominicans and Franciscans in the thirteenth century, also influenced the growth of scholasticism. The Dominicans, or Order of Friars Preachers, were devoted especially to preaching and teaching. Saint Dominic Guzman (d. 1221) founded the order to counter the Albigensian heresy. The Dominican school of theology, formed around Saint Albert the Great (d. 1280) and Saint Thomas Aquinas, was the leading school of the late Middle Ages.

Saint Francis of Assisi founded the Franciscans, or Order of Friars Minor, who were devoted to popular preaching and missionary activity. They promoted devotions such as the Angelus, the forty hours, the way of the cross and the Christmas crèche. The great popular preacher Saint Anthony of Padua (d. 1231) began the Franciscan school of theology and was the first teacher of theology to the friars.

Later outstanding teachers included Saint Bonaventure (d. 1274), who stressed the importance of the mystical illumination of the faithful by the Holy Spirit and the role of our will and our love in responding to the Holy Spirit, and Blessed John Duns Scotus (d. 1308), who taught and defended the absolute primacy of Christ and the Immaculate Conception of the Blessed Virgin Mary.

Two Currents of Thought Emerge

Beginning with the work of Saint Anselm, who stressed both faith and reason, two currents of thought ran through the scholastic period. The first was a spiritual or intuitive approach to truth. Based on the philosophy of Plato and rooted in the fathers, especially Saint Augustine, it later passed through Saint Bernard (d. 1153) and in the thirteenth century into the Franciscan school of theology. The Franciscan school, drawing information from its founder, stressed love and the way of the heart in the understanding and expression of God and divine realities.

The second trend was the logical or reasoning approach to truth. This current of thought, acknowledging the authority of the "proof of the fathers," grew increasingly strong. Assisted by the rediscovery of the ancient philosophy of Aristotle, with its stress on reason, this logical current finally predominated in the scholastic era, particularly in the Dominican school of theology. This stressed truth and the way of the mind in the understanding and expression of God and theological realities.

THE DOCTORS OF THE CHURCH

Doctors of the Church are the third group of special teachers whom the Spirit of truth has raised up. These men and women are not limited to a certain time or movement in the Church but are found interspersed throughout her long history.

Doctors of the Church must meet four criteria: they must have orthodoxy of doctrine, meaning that their teaching is clearly in conformity with Church dogma; holiness of life, since all are canonized saints; eminence in learning and excellence in teaching, having made a genuine contribution to the proper development of Church teaching; and a pope's explicit proclamation as doctor of the Church.

Pope Boniface VIII (d. 1303) proclaimed the first doctors of the Church in 1295. He declared that the four great fathers of the West—Saints Ambrose, Jerome, Augustine and Gregory the Great—were to be known as outstanding doctors or teachers of the Church. Pope Saint Pius V (d. 1572) declared the four great fathers of the East—Saints Basil the Great, Gregory of Nazianzus, John Chrysostom and Athanasius—as doctors of the Church in 1568. At present there are thirty-three doctors of the Church.

Formerly only male saints were named to this role. In 1970 Pope Paul VI (d. 1978) declared Saint Teresa of Avila the first female doctor of the Church. Soon after he added Saint Catherine of Siena to the list, and in 1998 Pope John Paul II added Saint Thérèse of Lisieux.

Many of the doctors of the Church have been given titles over the years. Some of these reflect their contribution to

Church teaching. Saint Augustine's title, Doctor of Grace, for example, reflects his vast contribution to our understanding of how grace works in our spiritual lives. Other titles might refer to the quality of the saint's writings: Saint Bernard of Clairvaux is called the Honey-Flowing Doctor (Doctor *Mellifluus*, in Latin) because his writings have a certain spiritual sweetness. Other titles refer to personal characteristics: Saint Thomas Aquinas is called the Angelic Doctor because of the great purity of his life and teachings. Saint Bonaventure is called the Seraphic Doctor because his writings have the ardor of the seraphim and because he was the first doctor from the order of Saint Francis, who is known as the Seraphic Saint because of the ardor of his love.

Growing in Wisdom Through the Light of the Holy Spirit

The doctors of the Church, known for their extraordinary holiness, drew the wisdom and light of the Holy Spirit from their own spiritual lives, chiefly through the deepening experiences of prayer. The *Catechism of the Catholic Church* recognizes that, though these experiences are not a part of the revelation contained in the deposit of faith, they do assist the magisterium in better understanding and proclaiming the truths God has revealed: "Thanks to the assistance of the Holy Spirit, the understanding of both the realities and the words of the heritage of faith is able to grow in the life of the Church: 'through the contemplation and study of believers who ponder these things in their hearts' [*Dei Verbum*, 8]" (*CCC*, #94).

Our Lady, the Mother of the Church, provides two outstanding examples of how meditation on God's Word can lead to a deeper insight into what He has revealed. Saint Luke twice refers to Mary's contemplation in her heart of the words and deeds connected with Jesus' childhood. In the first instance Our Lady reflected on the experience shared by the shepherds of Bethlehem on the night of Jesus' birth. They had seen a choir of angels who told them of the birth of the Christ Child. "But Mary kept all these things, pondering them in her heart"(Luke 2:19).

The second instance refers to the words that Jesus spoke to her when she found Him in the temple after a loss of three days: "Did you not know that I must be in my Father's house?" (Luke 2:49). Mary, not understanding His words, "kept all these things in her heart" (Luke 2:51). By her contemplative reflection Mary understood more deeply the mystery of her Son's divine relationship to His Father. Our Lady no doubt later shared her deeper understanding of Jesus' words and deeds with the Gospel writers.

The doctors of the Church drew wisdom from their own meditation and experiences. Saint John of the Cross, for example, in his book *Dark Night of the Soul*, tells us much about the struggles and purifications in the spiritual life. He drew heavily on his own personal experiences of such struggles and used, as well, Scripture, official Church teachings and the writings of the fathers, the scholastics and other doctors of the Church.[4]

The same is true of Saint Teresa of Avila in her writings on prayer. In her final book, *The Interior Castle*, her masterpiece on prayer, this great teacher of the spiritual life describes the soul's growth from its initial conversion to God all the way to the summit of holiness, called the "transforming union." She tells how the soul must pass through seven sets of dwelling places (usually called mansions) on its journey. She discusses the struggles in the practice of virtue in each mansion, as well as the type of prayer characteristic of each successive dwelling place. She is especially gifted at describing the work of the Holy Spirit in guiding the soul, particularly starting with the fourth mansion, when contemplative prayer begins.[5]

In all that she wrote, Saint Teresa drew substantially from her own experience of prayer in all stages of her spiritual life. In fact, Teresa tells us that God can give one or all of three distinct graces to a person regarding his or her own spiritual experiences.

First, a person can receive the grace of authentic prayer experiences but not be aware of their occurrence or their value. For example, a person can be going through the "dark night of the senses," with its characteristic prolonged dryness at prayer, and mistakenly conclude that he or she must have offended God and so been abandoned by Him.

Second, a person can receive the grace to understand an experience. This can come through a direct inner awareness from the Holy Spirit, through the explanation of a spiritual director or a teacher of spiritual theology or through a book or tape on the subject.

Third, a person may be given the grace to explain his or her experiences to others. Not everyone who understands an interior experience has the ability to express it meaningfully to others. Teresa of Avila had this and the other two graces, and her insightful writings on prayer are proof of this fact.

Will There Be More Doctors of the Church?

It seems certain that the Holy Spirit will raise up saintly men and women who will continue to make eminent contributions to the Church's understanding of the deposit of faith. Such a contribution could come, for example, as the explanation of a Church teaching being proposed as a defined dogma. Or someone might come forth as a teacher to combat a heresy. Or a saint might lead the Church in the ways of holiness through instruction. We can be sure that God will give us truly prophetic witnesses to the Catholic faith.

Some who might be declared doctors someday include Saint Louis Grignon de Monfort for his profound Marian teachings and Blessed John Duns Scotus for his defense of Our Lady's Immaculate Conception. More contemporary individuals include Saint Teresa Benedicta (Edith Stein) and Saint Padre Pio for their mystical teachings; Pope John Paul II, whose profound writings will affect the Catholic Church for the next century; Archbishop Fulton J. Sheen, a great evangelizer whose words deeply affected many; and maybe even Mother Teresa of Calcutta for her insights into the Church's universal role in salvation.

The future is in the hands of God. One thing we may safely say is that the fathers, the scholastics and the doctors of the Church will receive the great reward promised in Scripture: "And those who are wise shall shine like the brightness of the firmament; and those who turn many to righteousness, like the stars for ever and ever" (Daniel 12:3).

CHAPTER 12

Theologians and Their Role in the Church

THE WORD *THEOLOGY* COMES from two Greek words: *theos,* meaning "God," and *logos,* meaning literally "a word." In this instance, however, *logos* also means "an orderly or methodical presentation of something" or simply "the study of" some field of knowledge. The word *theology,* then, means "the study of God." It embraces the truths connected with God, including those known through nature but especially those known through divine revelation.

HOW AND WHEN THEOLOGY BEGAN

Theology emerged at the very roots of Christianity. The writings of the New Testament contain the heart of the Christian message. The Evangelists presented the words and deeds of Jesus Himself in their Gospel accounts. The letters of various apostles are the first attempts to explain the message of Jesus in more detail and apply it to the lives of His earliest disciples.

SAINT PAUL AND SAINT JOHN, THEOLOGIANS OF THE NEW TESTAMENT

Saint Paul and Saint John stand out as the most eminent theologians among the New Testament writers. Paul, the persecutor turned apostle, zealously preached the message of Jesus on his missionary journeys. He followed that up with his writings. These cover a wide range of thought: at one moment he is expressing some of the most profound teachings of Christianity, at another defending against heretical distortions of the truth, at still another addressing the practical moral problems that arose in the ecclesial communities he founded.

John, the disciple "whom Jesus loved" (John 13:23), stood below the cross of Jesus and received Our Lady into his care (see John 19:25–27). He became the theologian of the mystery of the eternal Word, who became flesh and dwelt among us (see John 1:1–14).

We might say that Paul was a teaching theologian focused on the care of his converts, while John was a mystical theologian focused on the contemplation of divine truth. The Church will always need these two emphases in those who carry on her work of theology.

THE APOSTOLIC FATHERS AND THE APOLOGISTS

The apostolic fathers preserve in their writings the teachings of the very early Church. The apostles themselves taught many of these men, and so their writings witness to what the Church believed and taught from the beginning. Their works form a significant part of "the proof from the fathers," witnessing to what the Church authentically understood and proclaimed of the message of Jesus.

During this period persecution of the Church began, particularly in the Roman Empire. Certain Christian writers rose up to defend the teachings of the Church against the arguments that pagan adversaries used to justify the persecution of Christians. These defenders, as we have seen with some of the fathers of the Church, were known as apologists. The work of defending the faith against heresy became a permanent part of the theologian's role over the course of the Church's history.

THE ROLE OF GREEK PHILOSOPHY

Theology as a systematic study and presentation of the teachings of the Catholic Church began when some of the early fathers attempted to explain the Word of God in Scripture and the simple truths of the Church. They reflected, for example, on the truths found in the Apostles' Creed, which dates back to the first Christian century. Around the end of the second and the beginning of the third Christian centuries, we witness the first use of Greek philosophy as an instrument to help explain the basic truths contained in the deposit of faith. The early fathers of the Church borrowed words like person and nature to explain the mysteries of the Trinity[1] and the Incarnation.[2]

Christian schools emerged for deeper study of the faith. Origen, for example, the great Scripture scholar who headed the first Christian school at Alexandria, drew upon Neo-Platonist philosophy. He applied the Neo-Platonist understanding of man—composed of body, soul and spirit—to his parallel understanding that Sacred Scripture has three levels of meaning: First, the *body* of Scripture presents the historical or literary sense of the events narrated or the meanings of the words themselves; second, the *soul* of Scripture presents a tropological or moral sense for applying that Scripture to daily Christian living; third, an allegorical or *spiritual* sense contains a hidden spiritual meaning.

THE EFFECT OF HERESIES

The many heresies that arose during the Church's first five centuries provided an important impetus to the development of Catholic theology. Fundamental truths were challenged. Macedonianism, for example, denied the divinity of the Holy Spirit. Nestorianism claimed that there were two persons in Jesus, a divine Person and a human person, and that Mary could only be called the Mother of Christ (the human person) and not the Mother of God (the divine Person).

These heresies challenged great minds in the Church not only to defend authentic teaching but also to explain that teaching more clearly and completely. Many of these fathers were bishops as well as eminent theologians.[3] Their works were confirmed by the magisterium of the Church—namely, the pope and the bishops who taught in union with him— often in the context of ecumenical councils.

TWO SIGNIFICANT THEOLOGIANS OF THE MIDDLE AGES

Theologians have played an important role in the Church throughout history. In medieval times, as we have seen, the scholastics contributed to the advance of theology. Saint

Thomas Aquinas' *Summa Theologica* was the crowning work of scholasticism and is still an invaluable aid in helping the Church better understand the content of revelation. Aquinas provided us with a thorough and clear systematic understanding of Church teaching.

Other theologians provided explanations for difficult issues, paving the way for certain doctrines to be accepted as official Church teaching. Blessed John Duns Scotus (d. 1308), for example, satisfactorily explained the classic objection to the teaching of the Immaculate Conception: "If Mary did not have original sin, and Jesus redeemed everyone, how was Mary redeemed by Christ?" Scotus answered that Jesus "pre-redeemed" His mother by preserving her beforehand from original sin in the light of the foreseen merits of His redemptive death. Thus Mary was both redeemed and free from original sin at the same time. This opened the way to the eventual proclamation of the great dogma of the Immaculate Conception of Our Lady.

THE ROLE OF THEOLOGIANS TODAY

There are three major aspects of the role of theologians. First, they explain the teachings of the Church. When we say that faith seeks understanding, we mean that we already accept the truths of the Catholic Church by a faith that believes before it fully comprehends. But our inquisitive minds want to grasp the truths of the Church as completely as possible. We will always need teachers who can make these truths more understandable.

Second, there will always be a need to defend the truths of the Church against objections, which arise in every age.

Third, theologians help the Church present her truths in such a way that they will influence the culture of different times and places.

The work of theologians, when properly carried out, is an important source of vitality for the life of the Catholic Church. In his *Testament* Saint Francis expresses his high regard for these teachers: "We should honor and venerate theologians, too, and the ministers of God's word, because it is they who give us spirit and life."[4] Theologians minister through a special grace that the Holy Spirit gives for the common good of the Church.

The Instruction on the Ecclesial Vocation of the Theologian states,

> Among the vocations awakened…by the Spirit in the Church is that of the theologian. His role is to pursue in a particular way an ever deeper understanding of the Word of God found in the inspired Scriptures and handed on by the living Tradition of the Church. He does this in communion with the Magisterium which has been charged with the responsibility of preserving the deposit of faith.[5]

Because the Church directs the role of theologians, they must be distinguished as loyal sons and daughters of the Church. We can see the ecclesial character of their vocation in two ways.

Of the Church

Before all else, the theologian must be a believer, someone who accepts in mind and heart whatever the Church's teaching authority defines, or at least proposes for belief, in the areas of faith and morals. The position of theologian does not exempt men and women from this belief, as some theologians have tried to claim in recent years under the pretext of academic freedom. Faith in what the Church already clearly teaches is the starting point for theological study; this is not the place for theologians to substitute their opinions for Church doctrine. This is why Origen insisted that his theology students follow the "rule of faith," adhering to that which had been handed down from the apostles and not disregarding or contradicting it.

Origen also demanded that his students observe a daily schedule of prayer. He knew that prayer would strengthen the faith needed to pursue the study of truth. There is a necessary link between holiness and faithfulness, as the *Catechism* tells us: "There is an organic connection between our spiritual life and the dogmas. Dogmas are lights along the path of faith; they illuminate it and make it secure. Conversely, if our life is upright, our intellect and heart will be open to welcome the light shed by the dogmas of faith" (#89).

A strong prayer life is one of the best means for theologians to maintain their personal orthodoxy of belief as well as orthodoxy in teaching the faith to others. As faith increases, so will the strength of conviction with which theologians teach and defend the doctrines of the Catholic Church. This is in keeping with an old saying, "One person with a belief is equal in force to ninety-nine who merely have an interest!" We need believing theologians in the Church today.

The Church requires those who teach theology in Church-related institutions to have a "mandate" from the

Church.[6] This mandate requires that the teacher of theology take an oath to faithfully teach authentic Catholic doctrine. The local bishop has the obligation to see that those who are required to take the oath take it and keep it.

For the Church

Theology begins when reason is applied to the deposit of faith found in Sacred Scripture and Tradition. In the process theologians offer greater insights into the meaning of revealed truths or reasons why these revealed truths should be believed. They apply these truths to the constantly changing needs and circumstances of the faithful and defend Church teaching when it is under attack.

Theologians place the fruits of their research at the disposal of the Church's magisterium, so that the magisterium can teach the faithful with greater clarity and spiritual profit.[7] This distinction led Saint Augustine to state: "What then we understand, we owe to reason; what we believe, to authority."[8] Authority refers to the Church's magisterium, or the pope and the bishops who teach in union with him, and reason is a reference to the insights of theologians.

The Church's magisterium could preserve the deposit of faith without the aid of theologians, but it could not go from a simple belief in these Church teachings to a more profound understanding of them without the help of theologians. The magisterium and the theologians, then, must collaborate in the work of evangelization. This is why Saint Augustine held that theologians are agents by which Christ guards His Church from error and makes it grow in truth.

PITFALLS ALONG THE THEOLOGIAN'S PATH

The role of theologians is not without challenges and even pitfalls. Sometimes these can be traced to questionable motivation, a bad attitude or lack of fidelity to official Church teaching. Let's look at some of these negative influences that can affect the theologian.

Richard Rolle (d. 1349), a late medieval mystic from Hampole, England, became disaffected with theologians after studying at Oxford in England and the Sorbonne in France. He observed that an old woman can be "more expert in God's love, and less in worldly pleasure, than the great divine, whose study is vain." This is true of the theologian who studies "for vanity…, that he may appear glorious and so be known, and may get rents and dignities." Thus he "is worthy to be held a fool, and not wise."[9]

Rolle's criticism probably has both merit and fault, but his words help us recognize some distinct dangers for theologians.

The Temptation of Vanity

Learning has a way of puffing some people up with pride. Saint Francis recognized this danger when he cautioned his friars in his rule that they were not to be anxious to learn from books or in school. Above all they were to seek to have the Spirit of the Lord and His working within.[10] The wisdom that comes from the Holy Spirit leads to a real grasp of the truth but does not induce pride. Wisdom lacks the intellectual finesse that so easily feeds a person's ego. This does not mean we should avoid studies! It does mean we must beware of making a vain display of our learning, flaunting it boastfully.

Disdain of Others

Educated people can also be tempted to look down on persons less educated, especially simple people like the old woman Rolle mentions. The Pharisees and scribes in the Gospels displayed such intellectual disdain and snobbery.

A case in point is that of the man born blind (see John 9). The Pharisees believed that if a person was born disabled, as the blind man was, then either he or his parents must have sinned to cause this disability. But Jesus said to His apostles, when they asked Him about this, that neither the man nor his parents had sinned. Rather, the man was born blind so that God might manifest His glory when Jesus healed him.

Once healed, the blind man believed in Jesus, but the Pharisees, who could see physically, were blind in their attitude toward Jesus. They missed this stupendous miracle over their petty concern that Jesus had violated the law by performing a miracle on the Sabbath. They focused on the tiny incidental fact that He made mud on the Sabbath, smeared the man's eyes with it and then told him to go and wash it off. Later on, when the former blind man asked the Pharisees and scribes if they wanted to become Jesus' disciples, they responded to the man scornfully and abusively: "They answered him, 'You were born in utter sin, and would you teach us?' And they cast him out" (see John 9:34). That is intellectual pride and disdain!

True theologians should have the attitude of true Christians. They should approach each person, learned or simple, with respect for his or her God-given personal dignity and not with an attitude of superiority. The unnecessary use of technical terminology or erudite vocabulary can be a means of intimidating others.

Furthermore, theologians should approach their studies in a humble spirit of reverence before the eternal truths that God has revealed. We are all novices in the school of God. Saint Thomas Aquinas had a mystical experience while writing his *Summa Theologica* and abandoned the work, never completing it. He said that compared to what he had just experienced, all he had written was straw!

The Idol of Reputation

Richard Rolle mentions reputation as a hazard for theologians. A person who consistently produces significant work, whether in writing or by preaching or teaching, eventually will catch people's attention. Theologians in this category will almost certainly gain a reputation for their ability. They are quite different, however, from someone who sets out to gain a reputation so that he can simply appear important to others.

Those who are ambitious for a reputation fall prey to two dangers. One is that they may be tempted to twist the truth to suit "itching ears" among their followers. They may succumb to the allurement of the praise of men rather than seeking the glory of God (see John 12:43). People who too highly esteem their own reputation lose the freedom to pursue and profess the truth. They wonder what people will think of them. They check the latest surveys to see which way the theological wind is blowing. Above all, they don't want to offend or, worse still, alienate friends who look up to them. They are, in other words, politically correct in regard to their theology.

Our Lord always spoke the truth, whether popular or not! Even His enemies acknowledged that He did not cater to human favor (see Luke 20:21). If a theologian wants to be faithful to his task in the Church, he must be free to teach the truths that will set others free.

A second danger for theologians who are overly concerned with their reputation is a feeling of such superiority and security that they will not allow anyone, even the Church's magisterium, to censor them or criticize their teachings. Basking in the limelight can lead to intellectual pride. In recent years this attitude has led some to assert that there is a new magisterium or teaching authority in the Church, equal with the teaching magisterium of the pope and the bishops in union with him. This parallel magisterium is referred to as the "magisterium of the theologians." It reduces the role of the pope and the bishops to that of theologians who are simply teaching their own opinions! It denies the special guidance of the Holy Spirit attached to their divinely established office.

Pope John Paul II strongly denounced such a notion of a parallel magisterium of theologians:

> Today we must note a widespread misunderstanding of the meaning and role of the Church's Magisterium. This is the root of the criticisms and protests regarding its pronouncements, as you have particularly pointed out with respect to the reactions in not a few theological and ecclesiastical circles to the most recent documents of the papal Magisterium....
>
> In this regard, it is certainly necessary to distinguish the attitude of theologians who, in a spirit of cooperation and ecclesial communion, present their difficulties and questions, and thus positively contribute to

the maturing of reflection on the deposit of faith, from the public stance of opposition to the Magisterium, which is described as "dissent"; the latter tends to set up a kind of counter-magisterium, presenting believers with alternative positions and forms of behavior. The plurality of cultures and of theological approaches and systems themselves has its legitimacy only if the unity of faith is presupposed in its objective meaning. The very freedom proper to theological research is never freedom with regard to the truth, but is justified and realized when the individual complies with the moral obligation of obeying the truth presented by Revelation and accepted in faith. [11]

Theologians are obliged to accept the teachings of the Catholic Church with an assent of mind and heart, both those directly defined by the pope and the bishops as well as other truths definitively proposed by the Church regarding faith and morals. These other truths, though not explicitly defined, are of utmost importance since they are necessarily connected to divine revelation, and thus the pronouncements about them necessarily fall under the Church's divinely established teaching authority.

The Lure of Material Gain

Rolle also mentions that some theologians function as such primarily to "obtain stipends and official positions." Recognition as a theologian can be a source of substantial income, especially from talks at conferences and royalties from books and tapes. This can affect the quality of a theologian's work, especially if theologians write to meet the demands of publication schedules. Furthermore, the lure of profit may cause them to compromise their integrity.

Stipends may also symbolize the lifestyle of the theologian. In the Christian life there is an intimate connection between one's living and one's believing. How theologians live will necessarily influence and even determine what they think, what they ultimately express as their beliefs and what they end up teaching others.

"You Can Tell a Tree by Its Fruit"

As Jesus teaches us, when the tree is good, its fruit is good (see Matthew 7:15–20). Living a vital Christian life will sustain clarity of vision, allowing theologians to remain open to the presence and working of the Holy Spirit. They will remember their obligation to be faithful to authentic Church teaching while maintaining an honest and balanced openness. This attitude of faithful enquiry allows them to explore the meaning of these revealed truths and seek answers to questions that have been raised. Those who avoid the darkness caused by intellectual pride and the allurement of sin will be able to operate most securely in the light of the Holy Spirit.

On the other hand, if a theologian is living in contradiction to true Christian morality, it will ultimately reveal itself through his theology. For a number of years, for example, the Vatican called into question the works of a well-known theologian. He eventually left the Church, his religious order and the priesthood! When he left, he frankly admitted that he had had a girlfriend for the previous ten years. One can only imagine how his lifestyle, obviously in conflict with his religious and priestly celibacy, were influencing the way he thought. How many people, duped by his sincerity, followed his distorted teachings? He betrayed his call as a theologian in the Church. In this case the fruit was not good because the tree was not good.

The role of the theologian is clearly an important yet challenging one. This is true for all called to a teaching role in the Church, from the magisterium on down. But despite its dangers and its burdens, it is a most vital part of her mission on earth. If those who teach are faithful in living the gospel message in their own lives and in proclaiming it to others, they will receive a great reward from the Lord in His kingdom. "You are the salt of the earth," the Lord said. "You are the light of the world." Whoever fulfills and teaches all that God commands "shall be called great in the kingdom of heaven" (Matthew 5:13, 14, 19). 🕊

CHAPTER 13

The Universal Ministry of Teaching: A Gift in the Church

JESUS, WHO TAUGHT CONSTANTLY during the three years of His public ministry, spoke in a way that kept His audience "spellbound" because "he taught them as one who had authority, and not as their scribes" (Mark 6:2; Matthew 7:28–29). He recognized that people were hungering to hear God's Word and there was no one to teach them: "They were like sheep without a shepherd" (Mark 6:34). The prophet Isaiah had foretold that He would "bring good tidings to the afflicted" (Isaiah 61:1; Luke 4:18).

Our Lord wanted all of His followers to teach as well, taking into account their circumstances and talents. He told His disciples that they must be "the salt of the earth" and "the light of the world" (Matthew 5:13–14). What do these images of salt and light mean?

THE SALT OF THE EARTH

In biblical times salt was a very precious item. Roman soldiers, for example, received half their salary in salt. The connection between salt and pay is even reflected in the fact that the word for salt in Latin, *sal*, is the root of our word *salary*. Salt was important in the ancient world because of its preservative and flavoring effects.

Salt Preserves

Before refrigeration people used salt to preserve food from decay. Salting certain foods heavily—especially meat and fish—extended their shelf life. We can see how the image of salt applies to the teaching mission of the Church. Faithful teaching helps to preserve the Catholic faith, keeping it free from error. It doesn't permit essential elements of God's revelation to be lost or distorted. When we preserve these truths of the Catholic faith by believing them, living them and handing them on to others, we—and what we teach—are "the salt of the earth."

Salt Enhances Flavor

Salt was and still is necessary to season foods, in order to bring out their natural flavors. Salt gives a sharper taste, a tang, to the foods we enjoy. When we eat food prepared without salt or some other appropriate seasoning, the food tastes dull, bland and unappetizing.

The meaning of Our Lord's comparison is simple. Just as salt is necessary to make food appetizing and attractive so that people will want to eat it, so Christian teachers must make their message attractive so that people will not only hunger for the Word of God and the truths of the Church but also willingly receive them.

However, if the salt goes flat, it is to be thrown out as useless (see Matthew 5:13). Teachers who distort Church teaching or betray it—either through bad example or neglect—must be replaced by those who will carry out the task faithfully.

THE LIGHT OF THE WORLD

Light, in Scripture, often refers to understanding, clarity and above all truth. When Jesus calls the disciples "the light of the world," He is not referring to physical light but to their role in bearing the light of His truth in the world. He Himself is the primary light—"I am the light of the world" (John 8:12a)— and He is the only source of true light. He gives His light to all who believe in Him: "He who follows me will not walk in darkness, but will have the light of life" (John 8:12b).

Saint Bonaventure explained this relationship of Jesus with His disciples by comparing Jesus to the sun, which is the source of its own light, and comparing the Church—the faithful in Christ—to the moon, which has no light of its own but receives light from the sun and reflects that light upon the earth. The Church must receive the light of truth from Jesus. Then, just as the moon has phases, the Church will mirror the light of Jesus into the world, more or less intensely, by the holiness of its members, its corporal and spiritual works of mercy and its mission of evangelization.

Light Versus Darkness in Secular Society

Spiritual darkness abounds in contemporary life. Ours is often described as a post-Christian society, meaning one that once accepted Christian values regarding life, honesty, sexuality, marriage and human dignity but has fallen into corruption. In fact, as secularism replaces society's foundation of Christian values, there is an increased bitterness toward anything Christian, especially the Catholic Church. Religious rights are restricted, and traditional Christian values regarding life and marriage are attacked. Pope John Paul II called this spiritual warfare between the forces of light and darkness a struggle between truth and anti-truth!

The Struggle of Light and Darkness Within the Church

Signs of this spiritual darkness can be seen even in the Church, a result of the widespread ignorance of the faith among so many Catholics today. Some of the young, especially those who grew up in the unstable period after Vatican Council II, have never received proper instruction. Others appear to have forgotten even the most elementary teaching they once received.

This lack of basic knowledge is compounded by many errors held even by devout Catholics. Many are confused by fundamentalist attacks on essential Catholic doctrines. For example, fundamentalists claim that the Holy Eucharist is only a symbol. They accuse Catholics of worshiping Mary as a goddess. They reject the Books of Maccabees with their reference to purgatory and then wonder, "Where is purgatory found in the Bible?" And with regard to the communion of saints, pray directly to God, they say, never through the intercession of others.

Distortions of the Catholic Church's history and doctrine abound. The media portray the Church in very negative terms in movies, books, magazines and newspapers. Favorite targets of this revisionist history are the Inquisition, the Crusades and the lives of scandalous popes. And now the media freely attack the Church over the clerical sex abuse cases, stereotyping nearly all priests as pedophiles or potential pedophiles.

All of these factors and more make it necessary to re-evangelize Catholics in the basics of their faith. More urgently than ever, loyal and learned Catholics must bring the light of Christ into the world! We need the Paraclete, the Spirit of truth, to come upon the Church once again in a new Pentecost that will renew the face of the earth.

THE CHURCH'S MINISTRY OF TEACHING

The Catholic Church carries out her teaching mission in many ways. In his apostolic exhortation "Catechesis in Our Time," Pope John Paul II stressed the shared but different responsibility of all Catholics, clergy and lay, to teach the faith:

> Catechesis always has been and always will be a work for which the whole Church must feel responsible and must wish to be responsible. But the Church's members have different responsibilities, derived from each one's mission. Because of their charge, pastors have, at differing levels, the chief responsibility for fostering, guiding and coordinating catechesis. For his part, the Pope has a lively awareness of the primary responsibility that rests on him in this field: In this he finds reasons for pastoral

concern but principally a source of joy and hope. Priests and religious have in catechesis a pre-eminent field for their apostolate. On another level, parents have a unique responsibility. Teachers, the various ministers of the Church, catechists, and also organizers of social communications, all have in various degrees very precise responsibilities in this education of the believing conscience, an education that is important for the life of the Church and affects the life of society as such.[1]

RELIGIOUS MEN AND WOMEN AS TEACHERS

When many adult Catholics think about their primary and secondary religious education, they remember the priests and the religious men and women who taught them. In the quote above, Pope John Paul II clearly stated the importance of these consecrated persons as teachers of religion: "Priests and religious have in catechesis a pre-eminent field for their apostolate." We have already considered the role of priests as teachers; here let us reflect briefly on the significant role of religious men and women.

The Holy Spirit has moved these religious to express their dedication to the Lord and His Church in various forms. The hunger and thirst of the body are more obvious and immediate needs than those of the soul, and so many religious, like the Missionaries of Charity and the Little Sisters of the Poor, are dedicated to apostolates that meet these needs by the corporal works of mercy. In the order of importance, however, the hunger of the soul for truth and understanding of God's revelation takes a logical priority over the hunger of the body for physical nourishment. This is why Saint Peter and the apostles would not abandon the ministry of the Word of God to serve even poor widows at table (see Acts 6:1–6). So the Holy Spirit has directed many religious to the ministry of teaching the faith to the young and even the not so young.

As we have seen, from earliest times in the Church's history there have been Christian centers of learning as well as outstanding teachers among the fathers and doctors of the church. Beginning in the sixth century monastic schools attached to various monasteries became numerous. We see the greatest expression of religious in the field of Christian education, however, in the rise of the many teaching communities from the sixteenth century onward.

The Holy Spirit raised up these communities of men and of women dedicated to imparting the knowledge of the Catholic faith as well as forming the young in the discipline of a Christian moral life. Some of these communities formed the basis of the Catholic school system that emerged in the United States during the nineteenth century. These religious have touched countless lives, leading people through the pilgrimage of faith in this world to the fullness of eternal life in the next!

THE LAITY EXERCISE THE MINISTRY OF TEACHING

Whether a mother is teaching her children their first prayers, or teenagers are sharing with their friends what they learned on a weekend retreat, or a young adult is teaching a religious education class about the Ten Commandments, or a college professor is lecturing on the sacraments, or a faithful theologian is writing on some special point of Catholic doctrine, all are participating in the teaching ministry of the Church today. These teaching opportunities are all open to the laity; in fact, the laity almost exclusively carry out the opportunities that are situated within the family setting.

Parents as teachers. The first Christian teaching takes place within the family unit. The *Catechism of the Catholic Church* describes the Christian family as a "domestic church" with an "evangelizing and missionary task" (#2204, 2205). It is a "privileged community" where the spouses are called to "eager cooperation as parents in their children's upbringing" (#2206). "The family is the community in which, from childhood, we can learn moral values, begin to honor God, and make good use of freedom. Family life is an initiation into life in society" and the Church (#2207). The early Christian education received in the home will ideally serve as the foundation for children's Catholic faith for the rest of their lives.

Parents have a duty to nurture the life they bring into the world, providing for their children's physical, emotional and spiritual needs. As they give their children a simple introduction to the Catholic faith, they should impart truths and moral values in a way that the children are able to grasp. They must then reinforce that teaching through an active practice of the faith, leading by their example. In the Rite of Baptism of Children, during the blessing for the child's father, the celebrant says, "He and his wife will be the first teachers of their child in the ways of faith. May they also be the best of teachers, bearing witness to the faith by what they say and do!"[2]

Without doubt, the best and most effective teaching parents give is to simply attend Mass on Sundays and holy days, prayerfully, eagerly and joyfully. What an impact it makes on children when they go to Mass and pray with their parents in church! Sadly, many parents today just drop their children off and return home or go out for a quick breakfast somewhere. This sends a disturbing mixed message to children.

Parents also should create a Catholic cultural environment in the home, displaying some good religious art, including statues, to help cultivate the Holy Spirit's gift of piety. They should avoid extremes, so that the house doesn't end up looking like a religious goods store or a church. The home environment should also include prayer together, such as grace at meals, morning and night prayers or the rosary. Not only does such prayer honor God and the saints; it also strengthens family bonds.

Notable feasts such as name days and special religious occasions such as a child's first Holy Communion and confirmation are times to invite devout Catholic grandparents, relatives and friends to share in the celebration. If they cannot come, they can have a good influence on a child by sending a special greeting or gift to highlight the importance of the occasion.

Primary education. When considering what school their children should attend, parents should choose the one that will best prepare them to face life as adult Christians. They might even choose to home school, as do an increasing number of parents who are concerned with the religious training of their children.

Ideally grammar and middle school education builds on what has already been learned in the home. It introduces children to a systematic study of the faith, strengthening their initial reception of the gospel message. This study can take place either in the school setting, if it is a Catholic school, in the home or in religious education classes.

Young children are highly impressionable, with a sense of wonder and an openness to learning. Generally they don't resist such teaching and can readily be formed in attitudes of faith. A veteran vocations director of a large religious community once told me that if you want to sow the seeds of a religious vocation, talk to the youngsters when they are in the third grade! "They'll never forget it!" he said.

As children reach the important transitional period called puberty, they change not only physically but also emotionally, intellectually and spiritually. They might not see parents and teachers as all-knowing as they did when they were younger. At the same time they might begin to challenge many things, including religious truths they have always accepted. This could be partially the result of secular influences they absorb from the media or negative ideas they pick up from classmates. It goes without saying that the strong emotions adolescents experience sometimes bring them face-to-face with moral decisions they have not dealt with before.

Teachers must be able to challenge these young people as they move awkwardly into adolescence. The best starting points are the teachers' own sense of conviction along with clarity in presenting authentic Church teaching. Likewise teachers should be sensitive to the emerging questions and challenges these young people grapple with each day. In answering their questions, teachers should always speak the truth in love.

Secondary education. I taught high school religion for six years around the beginning of the post–Vatican II upheaval and was stunned to see how many of my high school seniors struggled with a profound crisis of faith. After twelve years of

Catholic education, many no longer believed. Their own interior conflicts compounded the situation, and their questioning became open rebellion, complicated by moral dilemmas and choices regarding drugs, drinking and sex.

Subjectivism in teaching made matters much worse. Religion teachers began to challenge and even reject Church teaching in front of students, often offering their personal views in place of the truths of Scripture and Tradition. A significant number of priests and religious among the religion teachers experienced vocational crises. The result was doctrinal and moral confusion!

Now, as I have already mentioned, we have to deal with the negative effects of sexual misconduct among some priests and the ensuing scandal in the Church. The young are hero worshippers, and in terms of religion, the saints are their greatest heroes. But they also need priests and religious to be living examples they can admire and imitate. When these living heroes fall for whatever reason, young people can grow discouraged and find the Christian ideal diminished.

Peer pressure also plays a role in the teenage crisis of faith. "There is no way I want to be seen in church on Sunday with my family," a teenager thinks. Or in regard to drinking or sex, "All my friends are doing it." The impulse to conform weighs heavily on some teens, who cannot bear to be different from the crowd and to stand alone on a moral issue. Our teenagers need the power of God's grace and the strength of conviction to take a stand for Jesus.

Teaching the Catholic faith to high school teenagers has always been a challenge. During crises of faith they often set aside their beliefs unless someone provides strong guidance that they are willing to receive. This is why faithful Catholic teaching is so critical during the high school years!

Frequently another crisis prompts young people to seek God, or they mature intellectually and emotionally so that they are free to open themselves once again to the presence of God and truth in their lives. Some teenagers arrive at this point during their high school years. They weather the storms and emerge with a mature Catholic belief and value system. Others achieve this breakthrough later, sometimes in college, often when they marry and have children. When this happens, their faith will be their own by choice.

Religion teachers on this secondary level must present their material clearly and with conviction! The students might not like what their teachers are telling them, but if they respect their teachers for being honest and understanding, a lot more will sink in than is apparent. The worst label a teenager could apply to a religion teacher is "phony." The teen thinks, "You're telling me this because you have to, but you don't believe it yourself!" I once heard a psychologist say that 65 percent of what you communicate to others is communicated in the tone of your voice! Think of it: the tone of your voice gives people a strong clue as to whether or not you believe what you're saying.

High school religion teachers must also teach with patience and trust. Patience is necessary because their young students may not have reached the moment of grace when God will call to them, break through their deafness and cast His light into their hearts to dispel their blindness.

He did just that in the life of Saint Augustine, a young man who experienced a terrible crisis of faith. Augustine summed up his journey of faith with a phrase that gives all of us hope: "You have made us for yourself, O Lord, and our hearts are restless until they rest in you."[3]

Trust is necessary because teachers do not teach only for the present moment. When we sow the seeds of faith, some take more time to put out roots, sprout, grow and bear fruit according to God's grace and the generous response of the individual who receives that grace. The moment of grace will arrive when God wants it to, which is not necessarily the moment in which the teacher is teaching!

Finally, at this secondary level it's very important that the study of religion not be a purely academic experience—that is, one in which the student simply gets a mark for his or her studies as in every other academic subject. Vital forms of religious experience need to be integrated into the educational process. Pope John Paul II, with his World Youth Days, demonstrated how important it is for young people to experience prayer, reflection, singing and conferences with other young people who are alive in their faith. Periodic retreats, eucharistic adoration, group recitation of the rosary, as well as social outreach to the poor, the sick and the underprivileged, will spark the young to a more personal encounter with Jesus Christ, the ultimate goal of our efforts.

The post–high school years. After the turmoil of high school, many young people experience conversions that lead them to know and experience Jesus. Obviously, there are still many young adults who do not have a personal encounter with Christ even though they will later on, even at the eleventh hour of life! No doubt a number are in danger of never experiencing conversion at all, and we must pray and sacrifice for them, as Mary requested when she appeared at Fatima.

For young adults who do have a vibrant relationship with Christ, pursuing college and university studies of the Catholic faith can help them become dedicated men and women for the life of the Church. This has certainly been the case for many Catholics in recent years who have emerged from solid Catholic colleges and universities to bring the gospel into every field of work. We must pray for good Catholic institutions of higher learning. We must also pray for loyal Catholic teachers who are proud of their faith, live it with conviction and teach it in such a way that it challenges the young men and women who will soon become our lay leaders in the Catholic Church.

Evangelists in the media. Pope John Paul II mentioned social communications as an important element of the Church's teaching mission. These media encompass the written word—books, newspapers, periodicals and such that keep the Word of God in print before the people; the spoken word—tapes and other recordings but especially ministry through the radio, which allows widespread dissemination of the gospel over the airwaves; and the televised word, which is not only heard but impressively seen.

One of the first and perhaps the greatest media evangelist in the Church's history was the late Archbishop Fulton J. Sheen. For twenty years, from 1930 to 1950, he was the voice of the Church every Sunday evening on *The Catholic Hour.* An estimated four million Catholics listened each week. For six years, from 1951 to 1957, he held an audience of about thirty million people spellbound every Tuesday night with his very popular TV show *Life Is Worth Living.* Aimed at all people of good will, not just Catholics, it dealt with issues that touch our everyday lives. He brought many people to God and many converts to the Catholic Church.

Archbishop Sheen was a man of prayer. He said that the power of his message came from his daily "holy hour" before the Blessed Sacrament. His words were filled with the power of the Holy Spirit. He is a great role model for all involved with evangelization in the media.

In a secularized society where God is purposely excluded, the media can still convey the message that God is present among us. In mission countries where there are not enough priests and catechists, radio and television allow many poor and isolated Catholics to hear the teachings of the Church and maintain their faith. In countries where the Church is persecuted, shortwave radio brings Christ's truth to the faithful. To shut-ins and those in hospitals and nursing homes, the media bring hope and comfort in their trials.

Pope John Paul II declared that the Holy Spirit is the principal agent of the new evangelization in the Church. Like a conductor of a grand orchestra, the Holy Spirit will harmonize all expressions of Church teachings to give honor and glory to the most holy Trinity and lead individuals along the path of truth and holiness. He will then help us shine that truth into the world to dispel the darkness with the light of Christ. Let us pray for a renewed outpouring of the Spirit of truth upon the people of God!

Notes

Part I: Jesus Gives Us the Truth; the Spirit Helps Us Understand It

Chapter 1: The Mission of Jesus and His Church: To Proclaim the Truth

1. There is a sense of irony and even sarcasm in the statement of Jesus' Jewish adversaries, "We are descendants of Abraham, and have never been in bondage to anyone." Actually the descendants of Jacob, Abraham's grandson, were at one time reduced to a state of slavery in Egypt. Moses was sent by God to free the Jewish people from slavery by the events of the Passover.

   Later the Jews were defeated by King Nebuchadnezzar and exiled from their land into Babylon (modern Iraq). They endured this lot for about seventy years. God then used the Persian King Cyrus to defeat the Babylonians and send the Jewish people back to Israel to rebuild their country.

Part II: The Spirit of Truth and His Mission in the Church

Chapter 3: Jesus Promises the Spirit of Truth

1. Because the other gospel writers had already given accounts of Jesus' instituting the Eucharist at the Last Supper, Saint John omits this in his account. Earlier in his Gospel he gives an explanation and the promise of the Holy Eucharist in Jesus' discourse about Himself as the "bread of life" come down from heaven (see John 6).

2. Interestingly, Pope John Paul II, in his encyclical letter on the Holy Spirit, *Dominum et Vivificantem,* frequently uses the title Paraclete in connection with other titles for the Holy Spirit, such as the "Paraclete, the Spirit of Truth" (61), the "Paraclete-

Counsellor" (62), the "Spirit-Paraclete" (64). Pope John Paul II, *Lord and Giver of Life: Dominum et Vivificantem* (Washington: United States Catholic Conference, 1986), pp. 122, 124, 128.

3. Our Lord's teaching on the role of the Paraclete is found in various places in the Last Supper account in Saint John's Gospel. Jesus kept coming back to this important theme at different points in His discourse. Therefore, we will notice both a bit of repetition in the teachings and a lack of strict systematic order in their presentation.

4. For a fuller treatment of this point, the reader may want to refer to the author's previous book, *The Holy Spirit: The Gift of God* (Staten Island, N.Y.: Alba, 1994), pp. 8–10.

Chapter 4: The Spirit at Work in the Early Church

1. The opposite of life is death. Medically we describe death in many ways; for example, as brain death. In philosophy and theology, however, the traditional manner to describe death is as the separation of the soul from the body. Since the soul is the inner source of the body's activity, when it departs, then the body is dead. It is lifeless. All its natural functions cease: the heart stops pumping blood, the brain ceases its activity, the cells of the body begin to decompose.

2. To be "God-fearing" does not mean to have servile fear of God's punishment, like a slave fearing punishment from a master. Rather it means the reverential fear of not wanting to offend God because He is all-good and worthy of all our love. Many God-fearing Gentiles were attracted to the monotheism of Judaism, as opposed to the polytheism frequently found in Gentile pagan religions, and to the obviously sound Jewish moral teaching, as opposed to the immoral permissiveness prevalent among the pagans. Many of these Gentiles did not become full converts to Judaism, however, because they were not drawn to other aspects of Jewish observance such as circumcision. Paul, in his missionary journeys, had a measure of success in converting these God-fearing Gentile believers to

Christianity, while he had relatively little success in attracting the Jewish people.

Part III: The Spirit of Truth Raises Up Different Witnesses of Truth

Chapter 5: "Apostles, Prophets, Evangelists"

1. Even today we use the title "apostle" to describe certain saints as "apostles" of a particular devotion they helped to spread or a way of life they exemplified. We call Saint Margaret Mary Alacoque, for example, the Apostle of the Sacred Heart; Saint Faustina Kowalska the Apostle of Divine Mercy; Saint Vincent de Paul the Apostle of Charity; and Saint Thérèse of Lisieux the Apostle of the Little Way of Spiritual Childhood.

2. The ministries of apostles and prophets are clearly referred to in an important early Christian document on morality and Church practice known as the *Didache* or *The Teaching of the Twelve Apostles,* a work written probably between A.D. 60 and 100. It seems that as the hierarchy of the various local churches became more firmly established—with the bishop and his clergy clearly in leadership—these more charismatic ministries of "apostles, prophets and evangelists" became less needed. These ministries as separate roles gradually began to disappear and were absorbed in great measure by the bishop along with his priests and deacons.

    In fact, the *Didache* describes tensions and even disputes between the local bishop with his clergy and these itinerant ministers, who were sometimes accused of stirring up trouble and causing dissension in the local communities.

    Another problem clearly spoken of in the *Didache* is the difficulty of distinguishing true apostles, prophets and evangelists from false ones. Saint Paul himself spoke of "false apostles" (see 2 Corinthians 11:13). Ultimately the *Didache* said that discerning true ministers from false ones depended upon two things. First, does their ministry bear lasting good fruit for the Church? Second, do these ministers live lives of authentic virtue? If the answer is "yes" to both, they are exercising true ministries; however, if the answer to either or both is "no," then they must be regarded as false ministers!

3. Pope John Paul II, *Redemptoris Missio* ("Mission of the Redeemer"), On the Permanent Validity of the Church's Missionary Mandate, December 7, 1990, p. 3.

4. Taken from Pope John Paul II's Homily at a Mass at Aqueduct Racetrack, Queens, New York, on October 6, 1995, 1, quoted in *Make Room for the Mystery of God* (Boston: Pauline, 1995), p. 48.

5. Taken from Pope John Paul II's Apostolic Letter *Tertio Millennio Adveniente* (Boston: Pauline, 1994), n. 45, p. 51.

6. These "sanctifying gifts" were traditionally referred to in theology as the *gratia gratum faciens*, "the gifts that make us pleasing" to God, because they help us increase in personal holiness.

7. See 1 Corinthians 12:8–10; Ephesians 4:7–13; Romans 12:4–8.

8. As an illustration of this point, Our Lord in his Sermon on the mount says, "Not every one who says to me, 'Lord, Lord,' shall enter the kingdom of heaven, but he who does the will of my Father who is in heaven. On that day many will say to me, 'Lord, Lord, did we not prophesy in your name, and cast out demons in your name, and do many mighty works in your name?' And then will I declare to them, 'I never knew you; depart from me, you evildoers!'" (Matthew 7:21–28). Prophecy, discernment of spirits and miracles are all charismatic gifts, but their possession does not guarantee holiness, which depends on our doing the will of God faithfully.

9. The traditional Latin title for these gifts emphasizes this point. They were called *gratia gratis data*, "gifts freely given."

Part IV: The Spirit of Truth Guides Those in Pastoral Office

Chapter 6: The Spirit of Truth and the Role of Pastors in the Church

1. John L. McKenzie, *Dictionary of the Bible* (Milwaukee: Bruce, 1965), p. 802.

2. McKenzie, pp. 802–803.

3. International Commission on English in the Liturgy, *The Rites of the Catholic Church*, vol. 2 (Collegeville, Minn.: Liturgical, 1991), p. 46.

4. Saint Augustine, Sermon 46, 1–2, CCL 41, pp. 529–530, in *The Liturgy of the Hours According to the Roman Rite*, International Commission on English in the Liturgy, trans. (New York: Catholic Book, 1975), pp. 255–256.

5. The sum total of all the truths God has revealed and that are contained in the two fonts of revelation—namely, Sacred Scripture and Tradition—is called the "deposit of faith." This deposit of the public revelation God made during the time of the Old Testament and the beginning of the New Testament period ended with the death of the last apostle. The Church cannot, therefore, add anything new to this public revelation nor take anything away from it. Her task, especially through the work of her pastors under the guidance of the Holy Spirit, is to preserve intact this deposit of revealed truths, to interpret them correctly, to safeguard them from all error and to proclaim and teach these truths faithfully to successive generations of the faithful until Jesus comes again at the end of the world.

Chapter 7: Pastors and the Priestly Office of Jesus

1. The *Catechism of the Catholic Church* (#1554, pp. 388–389) states:

   The divinely instituted ecclesiastical ministry is exercised in different degrees by those who even from ancient times have been called bishops, priests and deacons" [*Lumen gentium*, 28]. Catholic doctrine, expressed in the liturgy, the Magisterium, and the constant practice of the Church, recognizes that there are two degrees of ministerial participation in the priesthood of Christ: the episcopacy and the presbyterate. The diaconate is intended to help and serve them. For this reason the term *sacerdos* in current usage denotes bishops and priests but not deacons. Yet Catholic doctrine teaches that the degrees of priestly participation (episcopate and presbyterate) and the degree of service (diaconate) are all three conferred by a sacramental act called "ordination," that is, by the sacrament of Holy Orders.

2. In his encyclical *Mediator Dei* Pope Pius XII wrote: "It is the same priest, Christ Jesus, whose sacred person His minister truly represents. Now the minister, by reason of the sacerdotal consecration which he has received, is truly made like to the high priest and possesses the authority to act in the power and place of the person of Christ Himself" (*CCC*, # 1548, p. 387).

3. The Vatican II Dogmatic Constitution on the Church states:

In the person of the bishops, then, to whom the priests render assistance, the Lord Jesus Christ, supreme high priest, is present in the midst of the faithful. Though seated at the right hand of God the Father, he is not absent from the assembly of his pontiffs; on the contrary indeed, it is above all through their signal service that he preaches the Word of God to all peoples and administers without cease to the faithful the sacraments of faith; that through their paternal care (cf. 1 Cor. 4:15) he incorporates, by a supernatural rebirth, new members into his body; that finally, through their wisdom and prudence he directs and guides the people of the New Testament on their journey towards eternal beatitude. Chosen to shepherd the Lord's flock, these pastors are servants of Christ and stewards of the mysteries of God. (*Lumen gentium,* 21, par. 1)

4. Canon law clearly states the obligation of the diocesan bishop in the matter of abuses: "[The bishop] is to exercise vigilance so that abuses do not creep into ecclesiastical discipline, especially regarding the ministry of the word, the celebration of the sacraments and sacramentals, the worship of God and the veneration of the saints, and the administration of goods" (canon 392, paragraph 2).

5. Saint Augustine, Sermon 169, 13 in John Rotelle, ed., *The Works of Saint Augustine: Sermons,* Edmund Hill, trans. (New Rochelle, N.Y.: New City, 1992), part III, vol. 5, p. 231.

6. The close link between the power of the Holy Spirit and the forgiveness of sins is seen in the fact that Jesus conferred the Holy Spirit upon the apostles on Easter night at the same time that He gave them the authority and ministry to forgive sins: "'Jesus said to them again, 'Peace be with you. As the Father has sent me, even so I send you.' And when he had said this, he breathed on them, and said to them, 'Receive the Holy Spirit. If you forgive the sins of any, they are forgiven; if you retain the sins of any, they are retained'" (John 20:21–23).

7. A bishop is the ordinary minister of the sacrament of confirmation. However, a priest, either with the required permission or in certain circumstances (for example, when he is baptizing an adult convert), may also administer the sacrament of confirmation.

8. A priest who knowingly says Mass with mortal sin on his soul would be, of course, guilty of a mortal sin called a "sacrilege."

9. Saint Augustine: "And that which was given by Paul, and that which was given by Peter, is Christ's; and if baptism was given by Judas it was Christ's." *Tractates on the Gospel According to St. John,* Tractate V, p. 18.

10. *Da mihi animas, caetera tolle,* Saint John Bosco's motto in Latin, is included on the Salesian coat of arms. See Hugo Hoever, *Lives of the Saints,* rev. ed. (New York: Catholic Book, 1989), p. 55.

11. Saint Francis, "Testament" in Marion A. Habig, ed., *St. Francis of Assisi: Writings and Early Biographies* (Chicago: Franciscan Herald, 1973), p. 67.

Chapter 8: Pastors and the Kingly Office of Jesus

1. Isaiah the prophet has four oracles (or prophetic utterances) that refer to the "Servant of the Lord" (namely, Isaiah 42:1–4; 49:1–7; 50:4–11; 52:13–53:12). There were many interpretations during the Old Testament period as to whom these oracles referred to (for example, the prophet Isaiah himself, a contemporary person in Israel's history or even Israel itself as a nation). The New Testament, however, and Christian tradition see Jesus as the fulfillment of these prophecies.

2. Ronald Lawler, Donald W. Wuerl, Thomas Comerford Lawler, eds., *The Teaching of Christ: A Catholic Catechism for Adults* (Huntington, Ind.: Our Sunday Visitor, 1976), p. 206.

3. Jesus entrusted a specific authority to Peter.... The "power of the keys" designates authority to govern the house of God, which is the Church. Jesus, the Good Shepherd, confirmed this mandate after his Resurrection: "Feed my sheep." The power to "bind and loose" connotes the authority to absolve sins, to pronounce doctrinal judgments, and to make disciplinary decisions in the Church. Jesus entrusted this authority to the Church through the ministry of the apostles (cf. Matthew 18:18) and in particular through the ministry of Peter, the only one to whom he specifically entrusted the keys of the kingdom. (*CCC*, #553, p. 142)

4. "This college, in so far as it is composed of many members, is the expression of the variety and universality of the People of God; and of the unity of the flock of Christ, in so far as it is assembled under one head" (*Lumen gentium*, 22, as quoted in *CCC*, #885, p. 234).

5. Lawler, pp. 206–207.

6. *Catechism of the Catholic Church*, #896, p. 237. The first quote is from Vatican II's Dogmatic Constitution on the Church, 27; the second is from Saint Ignatius of Antioch, Letter to the Smyrnians, 8, 8; 6.

7. *Rites*, vol. 2, p. 75.

8. *Rites*, vol. 2, p. 75.

9. *Rites*, vol. 2, p. 74.

10. *Rites*, vol. 2, p. 73.

Chapter 9: Pastors and the Prophetic Office of Jesus

1. "The infallibility of the pope…is not the same thing as revelation or inspiration. It does not imply any special supernatural insight or wisdom. But it is a precious safeguard for the whole Church. Through the gift of papal infallibility the Holy Spirit guards the faith of the whole Church from error" (Lawler, p. 228).

2. *Rites*, vol. 2, p. 75.

3. *Rites*, vol. 2, p. 75.

4. Saint Augustine, Sermon 46.

Chapter 10: The Laity Share the Threefold Mission of Jesus

1. Canon 204, as quoted in the *Catechism of the Catholic Church,* #871, p. 231.

2. Renzo Allegri, *Teresa of the Poor* (Ann Arbor, Mich.: Servant, 1996), p. 80.

Part V: The Spirit of Truth and Those in Various Teaching Ministries

Chapter 11: Special Teachers in Church History

1. Irenaeus, *Against Heresies*, Book IV, chapter 41, 2.

2. Saint Vincent of Lerins, *A Commonitory for the Antiquity and Universality of the Catholic Faith against the Profane Novelties of All Heresies*, chapter 29, 77.

3. Vincent of Lerins, chapter 23, 57.

4. Saint John of the Cross, *Dark Night of the Soul* (New York: Riverhead, 2002).

5. Saint Teresa of Avila, *Interior Castle* (New York: Image, 1989).

Chapter 12: Theologians and Their Role in the Church

1. The Catholic Church teaches that in persons the Trinity is three: the Father, the Son and the Holy Spirit. In nature the Trinity is one. So we speak of three divine Persons, one divine nature.

2. The Incarnation is the belief that the second divine Person of the Trinity, the Son of God, became man. Thus He is one divine Person, with His divine nature that He possessed from all eternity now having also a human nature that He took to Himself when He became flesh in the womb of the Blessed Virgin Mary by the overshadowing of the Holy Spirit (see Luke 1:35). He is one divine Person with both a divine nature and a human nature.

3. Saint Augustine of Hippo (d. 430), considered the greatest of the fathers of the Church, is an example of a bishop-theologian who combated a great heresy. Pelagianism, initiated by a lay monk named Pelagius (d.c. 418), claimed that the human race was not raised to a supernatural state. This heresy denied original sin by reducing the fall of Adam simply to a sin of bad example for his descendants. It also held that actual grace was not necessary for salvation because humanity could obtain the remission of sin and follow the path of holiness by free will alone. For Pelagius, therefore, Christ's redemption consisted basically of His teaching and good example and not the meriting for us of the forgiveness of our sins and sanctifying grace. Saint Augustine knew from his own long and difficult personal struggle with passion and sin that original sin was only too real: he could not be set free by his own efforts alone, but only by the grace of God. It is no wonder he is called the Doctor of Grace.

4. Saint Francis, "Testament," in Habig, pp. 67–68.

5. Congregation for the Doctrine of the Faith, Instruction on the Ecclesial Vocation of the Theologian, May 24, 1990, paragraph 6.

6. Canon 812 says that "those who teach theological disciplines in any institutes of higher studies whatsoever must have a mandate from the competent ecclesiastical authority." The latter is understood to be the local bishop.

7. Pope John Paul II, in an address to the Congregation for the Doctrine of the Faith (November 24, 1995), entitled "Magisterium Exercises Authority in Christ's Name," stated:

    The continual dialogue with Pastors and theologians throughout the world enables you to be attentive to the demands of understanding and reflecting more deeply on the doctrine of the faith, which theology interprets, and at the same time, it informs you of the useful efforts being made to foster and strengthen the unity of the faith and the Magisterium's guiding role in understanding the truth and in building up ecclesial communion in charity.... To achieve this end, theology can never be reduced to the "private" reflection of a theologian or group of theologians. The Church is the theologian's vital environment, and in order to remain faithful to its identity, theology cannot fail to participate deeply in the fabric of the Church's life, doctrine, holiness and prayer. (2)

8. Saint Augustine, "On the Profit of Believing," p. 25.

9. Richard Rolle, *The Fire of Love* or *Melody of Love*, Richard Misyn, trans., book I, chapter 5.

10. Saint Francis, "The Rule of 1223," in Habig, p. 63.

11. Pope John Paul II, "Magisterium Exercises Authority in Christ's Name," address to Congregation for the Doctrine of the Faith, November 24, 1995, paragraph 4. The pope cites as examples of documents that some theologians have criticized: "the Encyclicals 'Veritatis splendor,' on the principles of moral

doctrine and life, and 'Evangelium vitae,' on the value and inviolability of human life; the Apostolic Letter 'Ordinatio sacerdotalis,' on the impossibility of conferring priestly ordination on women; and the 'Letter' of the Congregation for the Doctrine of the Faith on the reception of Eucharistic Communion by divorced and remarried faithful."

Chapter 13: The Universal Ministry of Teaching: A Gift in the Church

1. Pope John Paul II, Apostolic Exhortation *Catechesi tradendae* ("On Catechesis in Our Time"), October 16, 1979, 16.

2. Rite of Baptism for Children, in *Rites of the Catholic Church* (Collegeville, Minn.: Liturgical, 1990), vol. 1, p. 442.

3. Saint Augustine, *Confessions*, 1:1, Henry Chadwick, trans. (Oxford: Oxford University Press, 1991), p. 3.

Index

A

Abel, 59
Acts of the Apostles, 37
Adam, 59
Albert the Great, Saint, 129
Albigensian heresy, 129
Ambrose, Saint, 131
Amos, 49
Ananias, 31
Annunciation, 84
Anselm of Canterbury, Saint, 127–128
Anthony of Padua, Saint, 129
apostles, 37, 48–49, 51. *See also* individual apostles.
Apostolic See, 72
Aquinas, Saint Thomas (*Summa Theologica*), 128–129, 132, 140, 146
Arianism, 126
Aristotle, 128
Ascension Thursday, 28
Athanasius, Saint, 126, 131
Augustine, Saint (*On the Trinity*), 77, 79, 112, 126–127, 131, 132, 143
Averroes, 128
Avicenna, 128

B

Barnabas, 40–41
Barsabbas, 41
Basil the Great, Saint, 131
Bernard of Clairvaux, Saint, 130, 132
bilocation, 54
bishops, 36, 43, 70–74, 90–93, 96–100
Bonaventure, Saint, 130, 132
Boniface VIII, Pope, 131

C

"Catechesis in our Time," 155
Catherine of Siena, Saint, 131
Christ
    as good shepherd, 4, 59–63
    as Messiah, 33
    authority of, 18
    body of, as temple, 18
    commandments of, 23
    example of service, 24
    glorification of, 30
    joy of, 24
    mission of, 66–67
    mystical body of, 47, 68
    peace of, 24
    priestly office of, 68–70
    promise of Holy Spirit, 24–35
    promise of union, 24
    purpose of coming, 3–4
    resurrection of, 12–14, 15
    truth of, 3–9